GAS DRILLING
AND THE
FRACKING OF A
MARRIAGE

GAS DRILLING AND THE FRACKING OF A MARRIAGE

Stephanie C. Hamel

coffeetownpress

Seattle, WA

coffeetownpress

Coffeetown Press
PO Box 70515
Seattle, WA 98127

For more information contact: www.coffeetownpress.com
www.hamel.coffeetownpress.com

Photographs of the Hamel Family by Michelle Devens-Fitz
Cover design by Sabrina Sun

Gas Drilling and The Fracking of a Marriage
Lyrics from David Bailey songs used with permission

ISBN: 978-1-60381-114-9 (Trade Paperback)
ISBN: 978-1-60381-115-6 (eBook)

Printed in the United States of America

In memory of my dad, Joseph N. Corrao,
who loved the farm.

Acknowledgments

It will be difficult to thank everyone who has contributed, either by bolstering us while we were in the midst of our gas-lease dilemma, or by guiding the writing and publishing of the book. Some names have made it to these pages, but many others have not. Of the latter, I send my heartfelt appreciation to my long-time friend, Ms. Stephanie Harp, and also to my editor, Ms. Catherine Treadgold. I send a hug to Shelley Beck Ley and to other pals and sorority sisters who have encouraged me in this writing dream of mine.

It delights me to thank my Lehigh University connections: Dr. Ned Heindel, Dr. Natalie Foster and Dr. Pete Beidler, and I hope and expect that the spirit of Dr. Natalie Freeman, formerly of the University of Medicine and Dentistry of New Jersey, will be amused at my success. I express gratitude to Mrs. Leslie Bailey, who granted my request to honor the late Mr. David Bailey by quoting his music lyrics.

Table of Contents

Notes and Disclaimers

This true story, written first in diary form and from notes taken during telephone conversations, reflects a developing knowledge of the natural gas industry and the legalities associated with land ownership and gas leasing. This is the information that was available at the time; however, my *facts* may no longer entirely hold true and therefore should not be quoted as legal truths.

Secondly, at the time my story unfolded, there was little, if any, open public concern in Pennsylvania (PA) over the negative impacts of drilling for natural gas. Appalachian PA has a long history of mining other forms of carbon-based fuels; the historical presence of the gas industry had been in the northwestern part of the state, where shallow drilling does not fracture, or 'frack,' the deep shale layers. When this story was unfolding, 'fracking' in PA was in its infancy.

Several of the people involved in this story have requested anonymity. I have changed their names, as I did for the one person who did not respond to my request for permission to quote. An asterisk* indicates a name that has been altered for this story.

Finally, the views expressed by Frank McLaughlin III are his own and do not represent the opinions of either the NJ Department of Environmental Protection or Ramapo College.

Gas-Lease Dilemma

Live the questions now, and perhaps,
without noticing it,
You will live along some distant day into
the answers.

—Rainer Maria Rilke

E-mail To: Frank McLaughlin, NJ Department of Environmental Protection
"From: Stephanie Hamel" September 10, 2008

Dear Frank,

I cannot recall the correct spelling for 'dilemma,' but that is what I am swimming in, at the moment, not to mention a few days' worth of sick kids' laundry. Frank, I have no time today for formalities, so here goes:

Two weeks ago, Tom and I were offered $2,500 an acre to lease our natural gas rights up in Wellsboro. The whole of northern Pennsylvania is singing the Hallelujah Chorus because there is gas under our land and it is now economically feasible to drill. There is a well within 0.50 miles of my property and I listened to the drilling during my quiet, reflective time—HA!—this summer; there are two more wells within a two mile radius.

Everyone in the area is seeing dollar signs and is signing up as fast as the lease agreement arrives on the doorstep. Tom Hamel has the unfortunate luck of being married to the only one who regards this windfall as a curse. Frank, it is very easy for me to criticize unrestrained fossil fuel consumption, but it is much more challenging to put my money where my mouth is when a large sum of my money is at stake. I am determined, however, to protect my land.

So, if it was that simple, Tom could simply kiss early retirement goodbye, stop singing "Oh, first thing you know ol' Jed's a millionaire ..." and conclude that he married the biggest fool, but unfortunately, it is not that simple.

(Pardon me, I just had to fish two popcorn kernels out of Michael's mouth.)

Where was I? Oh, okay, so it appears that there is a "capture clause" in the law that makes it allowable for the gas company to deplete our subsurface gas and NOT pay for it, should we NOT sign a lease agreement for surface rights! So much for my "protection of the world" plan ... It won't come to any effect (picture a bulldozer running over a tiny wooden peg). We are still trying to figure out what to do, and what our best option is. (That is, do we become traitors and take the money, then buy a hybrid car and solar panels for the house? It still doesn't all add up for me, but it might be a way to salvage something.)

I would like to talk to you about geology, drilling theory and any other information you may deem pertinent to our decision. I need to learn about surface damage that has occurred at other drilling sites and where to get PA DEP [Pennsylvania Department of Environmental Protection] or EPA [Environmental Protection Agency] regulations ...

Could you help us?

Let me know when I can call you. Friday is no good; this weekend will be fine.

I'll be bugging you soon.

—Stephanie

I shouldn't have been surprised when a lease agreement finally arrived in the mail or that there was a difference in opinion in my own home as to whether or not to sign it. The controversy of natural gas drilling had carved its mark in my marriage earlier in the summer. Local rumor insisted that natural gas, lying deep in the Marcellus shale under our part of the world, was now accessible and that the energy companies were in a mad, mad race to snatch large tracts of land that they might lease for drilling. If the chatter was true, land agents and gas leases were flying to every homeowner in northern Pennsylvania.

My husband, who had been privy to the prevailing gossip of the golf course, enthusiastically adopted the possibility of easy money. His precarious job situation, combined with a normal human desire to have an enormous chunk of change stashed in the bank, had made him an enthusiastic proponent of gas leasing.

"Texas rich," he'd murmur, with a gleam in his eye. "We'd be Texas rich."

I, consumed with the parenting duties associated with young children, had neither time nor energy for such wild monetary dreams. Gas-lease fever may have struck Pennsylvania, but I was not going to be a victim of that disease. I snorted disdainfully whenever Tom broached the topic.

"Not on my land. Don't even think about it." After a pause I would add, "I don't want the land destroyed. My dad wouldn't have done it."

It had been my parents' land, and my childhood summertime memories are wrapped in its fifty acres. My own seven-year-old son, legs skinny and face aglow, races across the hilltop toward the barn, and I am struck by his knobby-kneed childhood gait, so similar to my own, and remember my father, his arms pumping as his long legs sprinted across that very field. In this transient era, few people have one location that links generations. Watching a living re-creation of memories, I realize what a treasure I have. Destroy it with gas wells? Never!

The lease conflict had led to a few vague arguments with Tom, resulting in our being rather miffed with each other; however, being purely hypothetical in nature, the discussions were quickly buried by other day-to-day joys and worries. When we arrived at the farm for our weekend visits and gas-lease talk surrounded us in restaurants, I silently congratulated myself for upholding the unique stance of placing the environmental welfare of the planet above monetary considerations. I, a scientist with all the credentials, knew better than to destroy the world by promoting fossil fuel burning.

"I would never accept such an offer," I was quietly convinced. Holding my head at a righteous angle, I greeted the receipt of a gas lease offer in the mail with an emphatic "No!" No need to destroy the land or develop it. Tom, on the other hand, had stared in amazement at the lease amount and could not dismiss the possibility. He saw a life of ease on the horizon, if only I would capitulate. Our quarreling escalated.

In the midst of our bickering, I began to research gas drilling and uncovered an old Pennsylvania statute from the oil or maybe coal mining days, nicknamed 'The Law of Capture.' While at first it seemed unfathomable, closer inspection confirmed that although I could prevent the company from drilling *on* my land, I could not prevent it from extracting gas from *under* my land, should it be drawn into a neighbor's well. My stomach flopped at the thought. My ability to protect the gas was legally non-existent. I could forego the money by ignoring a lease option, but that sacrifice might not prevent one molecule of gas from being captured and burned.

So much for saving the environment, I thought. Will I still act on principle? What on earth happens when acting on principle has no positive effect? Is an empty principle worth the fight?

Developing a Love of the Land

I am devoted to a small parcel of land in north central Pennsylvania. It isn't an ideal piece of real estate; indeed it certainly has an abundance of negative attributes. The property, mostly overgrown with goldenrod, sits adjacent to a busy roadway, and the house is settled too near the neighbor's overgrown hedge. The shape of the land and its topography make it impossible to get a decent view from the porch; only upstairs can we glimpse a smallish mountain across the valley.

Over one hundred and fifty years ago, when farmers first tried to eke out a living on the Appalachian plateau, the house was a starter home. Framed with hand-hewn logs, pegged into shape, it was floored and sided with wide hemlock planks. A quarter century later, a bigger home was constructed nearby, relegating the little post-and-beam building to house equipment instead of people. When the bigger farm prospered in the early twentieth century, two separate additions to the little house converted it into six rooms of living space for hired hands. It was lit by a few bare light bulbs and heated by a kerosene stove, and its walls were sided with yellow asphalt paper to repulse the drafts that sliced through its thin boards.

On a hot summer afternoon, my parents purchased the little house and fifty adjoining acres, for use as a summer 'camp,' as it is called here. I had slid off of the sticky backseat of the station wagon to wait alongside the car, while my parents introduced themselves to white-haired Mr. Penney. I was bored with this whole process of looking for a place. On the way to see a realtor, we had passed a 'Farm for Sale' sign, and my father had turned the car around. The sun beat down on my head as I absently began to pull seed tops off of nearby grasses. My little sister joined me in my task.

Mr. Penney took his time explaining that he and his wife had divided most of their hundred-acre rectangle of land into two interlinked 'L' shaped lots. Each included a small house and a large barn. He lifted a shaking arm to point to the lower half, which had recently been sold to "another 'downstater," and indicated that they, the Penneys, would retain the big house, in front of the little tenants' house, the latter being still available for purchase.

Mr. Penney paused to look in my direction. By then Natalie and I were filling little plastic milk jugs from the floor of the back seat with the grass seed. With a glimmer of a smile, Mr. Penney reached over to peel some seeds off of a stem.

"That's timothy." His voice was thick and heavy. "I was a seed dealer, and over the years the birds have stolen it from my piles up the corncrib and sowed it all over."

My brother dropped his book and climbed out of the car to join us as we strolled across the lawn to see the little house. It was ugly from the outside, with its 'fake brick' tar paper siding, its roof peak that did not follow the line of shed roof of the attached porch, and three unsteady steps leading to a floor of peeling white paint. A half-wall of multi-colored shingles—perhaps a railing—gave the odd impression that a portion of a roof had avalanched to the front of the porch.

Long bereft of farmhands, the inside had reverted to a storage area, and grass seed lay in enormous piles on the floors. "Timothy," I whispered to my sister, as we entered. Mr. Penney nodded.

The house was worse inside than out, with the lined plaster wallboard marked with water stains and cracked linoleum on the floors. Stifling heat assailed us. After a quick run upstairs, we were back on the sagging porch with my father extending his hand. My parents had bought the place. Mr. Penney would hold the mortgage and I would not have to sit in any more realty offices, their only magazines filled with boring house pictures.

During the first years of ownership, our visits featured repairs to the little house, with Mr. Penney hobbling over to offer advice and tools. Dad soon had water running into the little house; he upgraded the electricity to accommodate a hot water tank and salvaged an old oil burner.

My brother, Mark, pried rows of nails from the huge old timbers we discovered under the old wallboards and my mother wore rubber gloves as she scrubbed the massive beams with a bleach solution. The strange porch accoutrement of multi-colored shingles was discarded, and on a sunny Saturday afternoon we repainted the floor with fresh white paint. My siblings and I began to spend our summers learning to fix things: to shingle roofs, mix cement, and spackle sheetrock.

On weekends we climbed into the loft of our own barn, and scattered the grass seed found in the corncribs for our pretend chickens. Mr. Penney showed us the wild raspberry brambles and reported a recent sighting of "an ol' black bar." My sister and I were pleasantly frightened at the possibility of seeing one for ourselves.

We picked mint by the spring and caught tiny pollywogs in the neighbors' pond; mud squished between our toes as we waded in the muck. On hot afternoons, Natalie and I used the dark, damp springhouse as a playhouse. On the upland, Mark and I hacked away the scratchy brambles clinging to an ancient, dilapidated pickup truck. Decaying amid the tall weeds, its rusty doors could be wrenched open enough to allow us to climb inside. We bounced on the cracked leather seat, imagining we were steering and shifting; however, the cab was protected from the wind, allowing volatilized oils in the grease to permeate everything, and their stomach-grabbing odors caused us to try—in vain—to crank the windows open. When the smell became unbearable, we would clamor over the wooden sides to the truck bed, or run down the hill to find something new to explore.

When I lay on the lawn, the wind made funny sounds in my ears and I watched fluffy clouds separate the blue sky into different shades. I picked the prettiest blue. The sky was bigger, the land was wilder, and my imagination traveled so much farther here than at home in the suburbs.

There is probably little need, then, to state that I have a sentimental attachment to the place. Those childhood memories are really why it is mine today. There could be no other logical reason, after my father's illness and death, to purchase the property from my mother. The land—some wooded, some hayfield and the rest scrub—was not farmed, and the buildings were, by then, run-down and nearly worthless. Our farm's value was that it held many of the happy memories of my lifetime, and that was enough.

To the Farm

It's the life that I have chosen and I'll
suffer through my gain.

David M. Bailey, "Give me Your Today"

Wednesday, August 20, 2008

Finally, for once, I would be spending more than a week at
the farm. We had spent innumerable weekends here, but I
longed to lose the sense of urgency that surrounded these
short visits. I rubbed my hands together in anticipation: we
would loll, relaxed, under no time pressure, in no rush to
enjoy everything before having to leave.

It was going to be tiring, as Tom would be working and I
would be alone with the boys, but I couldn't wait to get
started, and Tom might even join us for Saturday afternoon
and Sunday.

It took a long time to get moving, for despite all of the
exercises to stretch my aching back muscles, I hobbled about
while I packed. Still, as I drove with the boys in the back seat,
I was so happy that I decided to take a side trip en route: a
visit to a little zoo. For years I had wanted to tour the place
but, despite passing it a thousand times, my parents had never
stopped. On those Friday nights it was always too late, and we
would whiz past, cramped in the old station wagon with all
the baggage for those two hundred miles. We were always
racing to get there, or to return to Philadelphia. Because the

turnpike narrowed to a single lane to enter the Lehigh tunnel, merging cars clogged the roadway. We had to beat the weekend traffic! As we sped past I would curiously glance through the car window at the wooden and screened animal cages.

Now, so, many years later—in charge of myself and the plans—I spent an hour with two excited little boys gawking at the snakes and Galapagos tortoises. It was nicer than what I had imagined all these years.

When we returned to the parking lot, the sun was ablaze overhead and the hot interior of the car smelled of gasoline fumes. The fumes that somehow entered the car were worst on hot summer days, especially after I filled the tank. There was, a mechanic had told me, a pinhole leak in the tank, at the top somewhere. He hesitated, not wanting to replace the tank for fear that other rusting metal parts would be irrevocably damaged in the process. I knew we needed a new car; the fumes couldn't be healthy for any of us.

Despite opening the car windows, the smell did not completely disappear, and I was sickish and headachy when we arrived at the farm a few hours later. The boys, however, seemed to feel none of my ill effects, and were happily racing out of the car as I, with droopy shoulders and squinty eyes, unlocked the front door of the 'camp,' flipped on the electrical switches, and opened a few windows. I left piles of bags strewn in the kitchen, stowed only the leftover meal items into the refrigerator, asked Matthew to watch Michael, and then flopped on the bed upstairs.

Luckily the boys were engrossed in their toys, so I lay for a long, long time before mustering all of my strength to supervise teeth cleaning and help them into their pajamas and beds. I then sprawled across the double bed in my room, getting up only to answer Matthew's call. He wanted me to see the spectacular sunset from his window. A gorgeous array of oranges, yellows and reds was splashed across the western sky. I was so happy he had noticed it, though I couldn't really enjoy the sight myself. I kissed him and crawled back into my bed.

In later hours of darkness, Michael whimpered and cried, so I pulled him onto my bed, and for a few hours he kicked and tossed. When I groggily realized that I was getting no sleep at all, I carried him back to his crib. At dawn, Matthew woke me when he crawled in beside me, complaining of being cold. My night's sleep was broken, yet I felt surprisingly and immeasurably better in the morning.

Opening the House

And a small cabin build there, of clay and
wattles made …
And live alone in the bee-loved glade.

W.B. Yeats, "The Lake Isle of Innisfree"

Thursday, August 21, 2008

I served the boys toast and juice for breakfast and then
drove us to town for more groceries. After my headache the
day before, I decided to make things easy, to do only one
errand each day, especially since I would be on my own as a
parent for so long.

"No big projects!" I kept reminding myself. "Nothing
new until Tom arrives."

This little house did require attention every time we
opened it, but the day before I had done only the bare
minimum. I could clean and tidy, I reasoned, after we
returned with the groceries. After all, the work needed now
was nothing compared to the chores that had awaited us upon
our arrival when I was kid.

ঌৡঌৡঌ

We never discovered why—and I have never made
scientific inquiries into the reason—that so many flies lived
and died in this little house. All I know is that there were

thousands of them dead on the upstairs floors when we would arrive on Friday nights, and others were buzzing around the suddenly bright light bulbs.

My mother soon reserved space in the car to transport a loud and ancient vacuum cleaner that had once belonged to my grandmother. Before she managed to squeeze the extra appliance into the station wagon, we ventured downtown one hot Saturday afternoon to shop for flypaper. Wellsboro, the seat of a rather remote Pennsylvania county, boasts an imposing courthouse, vintage gas lights lining Main Street and a well-tended village green, but no flypaper could be found. We instead purchased an unheard of number of flyswatters—five—and drove home to swat. We swatted and continued to swat, and, even years after the old vacuum clogged the night stillness with its deafeningly hollow monotone, we still attack the living flies with those swatters.

Fly removal, however, wasn't the first chore on those dark Friday nights. The car tires would crunch over the sparse pebbles of the driveway until it reached the tenants' house and Dad parked on the grass. The brushing sound of the grass against the bumper was an indicator of Saturday's lawn care chores, and the softness of the ground revealed a recent history of rainfall. We would quit the messy car to stretch and enjoy the chilly air—a relief after the warmth of the enclosed car. I would stiffly shift from one foot to the other, glad for the motor's silence. Starlight pricked the velvety black sky, frogs burped in the pond below, and our footsteps made a distinctive clopping sound on the rickety wooden steps.

I would hold the flashlight for Dad as he fumbled with the leather key wallet at the front door, and we would all wait while he turned on the flashlight and ventured inside. At the time it seemed a heroic act to me—Dad's entering such an empty, dark house.

After turning the corner of the living room, he could lift the hook and eye latch of the utility room door, open it, and walk to the electrical main switch.

When its snap resounded and light flooded from the bare bulb on the ceiling, he would deftly flip on other lamps. In the comfort of the light, my apprehension evaporated. Blinking, we'd trudge into the musty warmth of the house, our hands filled with those odd things that accumulate in a car—squashed paper tissues, a soda can, a book—each holding the door for the next person with foot or elbow.

Dad hurried down to the basement to prime the water pump. A galvanized bucket, half-filled with water, waited next to the pipe wrenches, but sometimes there wasn't enough water for the job. One of us would be summoned to take the bucket across the dew-damp lawn. There, under the green apple tree, the ground abruptly sloped to a little wooden springhouse.

Years of water damage had taken its toll on that gray building. The thin cement floor had cracked; the rotting bottom of the door was jagged against the doorsill. Sliding down the slippery wet grass, I would reach for the elegant, brown-swirled china knob, smooth under my hand and so out of place there. The knob was not even needed to turn the door, yet I held onto it for comfort as I unfastened a rusty metal latch and shone the flashlight inside the tiny building. One evening I startled a small snake, which promptly slithered away, and once we found a delicate, translucent snakeskin curved on the floor. I always looked for snakes.

The 'spring' is really a stone-lined well not more than six feet deep, yet by staring straight down into the blackness I could imagine it to be a hundred feet. As the rays of my flashlight pierced the surface, I saw a frog bend and scrunch, bend and scrunch his legs, then disappear under a crevice deep in its stone wall.

A dip of the bucket shattered the smoothness of the water; then, carefully—to prevent the bucket from sloshing cold water onto my legs—I walked across the lawn toward the shining light escaping from the cellar, my dew prints following me. There I would find Dad, crouching over the pipe to the well, adding water, paper cupful by paper cupful, until it overflowed at the juncture. After replacing the cap and tightening it with the littlest pipe wrench, he would stick his head up through the trapdoor in the utility room and holler, "Give it a try, men!"

It was always fun to be the one in on the action, running to switch the heavy handle of the electrical breaker then standing guard to flip it back, in case the pump's motor ran too long without being cooled by the flow of water. For all of us, it was a time to pause from unloading the car trunk, emptying the contents of the metal ice cooler, or sweeping the mouse droppings. We would listen to the sound of the intensity of the pump, hoping to hear a change in the pitch, a change in pressure. If the priming didn't succeed, we might not have water that night, and Dad would be spending the next day under the house with wrenches. Everything depended on whether the pressure rose. With a reassuring click and Dad's triumphant, "There she goes, men!" we would exhale and get back to unpacking. Tools in hand, Dad would happily offer to reposition the boards above the spring in 'the well house.' That was a relief to me. Outside was so dark, and a little scary; I would rather be inside, in the bustle.

From the squeaky spigots rushed rusty water that swirled down the drains for several minutes before running clear. The counters and sinks were wiped. We collected shoes, towels and clothes spilling from duffel bags and clumped up the narrow wooden staircase from the kitchen to the attic bedrooms. As we ascended, we were assaulted by stagnating hot air, our discomfort increasing with each step. When our heads popped level with the wide wooden floors, we would marvel aloud at the vast black ocean of dead flies on the floors.

Mom stepped gingerly over these dead flies to open the

old wooden-framed windows, one in each upstairs room. She inserted metal screens under the open windows to allow a cross-ventilating breeze. By morning, the heat would dissipate and the air would be chilled, but for now, sweat broke on our foreheads as we pulled thin plastic coverings from the beds and unrolled sleeping bags onto bare mattresses.

Live flies wakened to hum with erratic whines around the bare ceiling bulbs. From the top of the stairs, Mom would request a broom, dustpan and brush, and we soon had little black heaps all over the floors. Mark would begin the swatting in his little room and continue until bedtime, but the buzzing of flies was always hard to stifle.

Over the years, the swatters deteriorated, but two survived. Limp and tired though they might be, they are still our primary means of insect control. The piles of flies on the floor disappeared once the house renovations began a few years ago. Tom and I had to replace the water pump and the new water pump doesn't need to be primed at the start of each visit. Yet, still, every first evening upon arrival, we are relieved to hear the pump click, and can be heard calling from upstairs, "I need a flyswatter up here!"

ৰৢৢৢৢৢৢ

Now, on a morning decades removed from my childhood, it took over an hour to shop for groceries, because I kept stopping to pass juice, crackers, and bananas to my children in front of the cart. Still, I was so delighted to be feeling myself again that, after shopping, I impetuously pushed them and the cart, at top speed, careening wildly around the vacant lot behind the store. They screamed with delight as we passed the silent trailers, circumvented clumps of weeds, then slowed to enter the busy part of the parking lot. I paused, panting, near the car.

"No other mother," I gasped, "ever does that! You have

the only mother on the planet who plays like this." Exhausted, and feeling that I had already aggravated my bad back, I refused their enthusiastic entreaties to "Do it again, MOMMY, do it AGAIN!"

I helped Michael into his car seat, loaded the groceries, and, once home, stowed food in the refrigerator and cabinets. I wiped the kitchen counters, as I feared some live virus in the mouse droppings I had found there in the morning. We ate lunch and napped; then I vacuumed the floor and re-wiped the counters before heading outside. Matthew and I picked blueberries in the sun, while two-year-old Michael hit golf balls on the lawn near us. Most of his shots landed in the tall weeds, so I kept an eye on his hitting, to know where to search when he cried for the lost ones.

Much later, the sun slanted across the hall floor as I washed the kitchen counters again with hot, soapy water. Thinking proudly that I had managed a good dinner—and day—I heard a woman's voice at the screen door. Becky Dodson's face appeared. Becky is a professor of music at a nearby university; now everyone calls her 'Rebecca.' This woman—who in our college days pledged our sorority while reciting insipid jingles and wearing a baby blue jumper and beaky hat—will always be 'Becky' to me. Last year, I had been tickled to discover that she was living in town; today, she was making a surprise visit to dig bee balm from our overgrown patch. I was silently thankful that she hadn't appeared the evening before to discover me in a droopy, pathetic state.

I went to search for an old cardboard box for the plants, while Michael hit more golf balls across the lawn and Matthew located our shovel to help dig. Returning with a somewhat bedraggled cardboard box, I chattered to Becky, glad for the adult conversation. There aren't many neighbors here, and so we rarely see people when we come. Becky is an outsider, too, a 'flatlander,' as the locals refer to us, but she is now part of the fabric of the community, something that Tom and I are not. We arrive unheralded, stay just the weekend, and are mostly left to ourselves.

For thirty summers, we managed to conduct our vacation lives without a telephone, our guests arriving announced only by previously expressed intent. Farm business arrangements were performed in person. After my college years, I spent weekends alone here, and drove miles to town to call my parents or Tom from a pay phone on the village green. Distance from people—both from crowds and from our own connections—does remain one of the reasons we go to the farm, but we are not disconnected anymore.

We installed the first phone line when Matthew was a baby, agreeing that it would be prudent to have contact with the outside world in the event of an emergency. We had it switched on at Memorial Day and off after September. There were occasional miscommunications or troubles having the phone activated, so when Tom's new job came with a cell phone, we neglected the land line. The damage, however, had already been done. I groaned the first night when, sitting on the porch with our weekend company, Tom took a phone call—nothing important, just a chatty call from his mother. Not that I don't love my mother-in-law, but it was a harbinger of a loss. A distinction that once existed was suddenly and irrevocably gone. We could be reached, even on vacation, for any reason.

Cell phones now allow us continuous contact with others, and while these phones promote security, they interfere with 'getting away from it all.' I have fought the tendency to have constant communication. It was only last winter, when I had sudden car trouble, that I bought a simple cell phone for emergencies. I have never learned the number, and would have difficulty accessing it without a manual. People assume that working for years in laboratories and running instruments with state-of-the-art technologies makes me adept at working electronic devices. Becky was amused when I mentioned that I didn't know my cell phone number. I suppose that in some peculiarly passive way, I am simply trying to retain a little of what I once had: seclusion.

Lately though, I've felt that my success has been double-edged, especially at the vacation spot. When I was a child visiting the farm, my family was here with me to provide any desired companionship that I might want. As an adult in the working world, I found relief in a weekend away from other people. Now, with so few adults in my life, I am lonely at times for intelligent communication, and thus feel even more isolated here at the farm. I extended an offer to Becky to return without any prior notice. She laughed, accepted and, with a box of shaggy red bee balm in the backseat of her car, disappeared.

Quiet Stillness and Noisy Motion

Love the time it takes to find the truth,
Love the time you dance with the mystery,
Love the wisdom of the old and the vision
of the youth.

David M. Bailey, "Love the Time"

Dehydration, from the heat I supposed, had rendered Matthew bleary-eyed and apathetic, so we spent most of the next day lolling on the porch, in the shade, with me reading story after story to the boys. Road noise zapped some of the pleasure: motorcycle convoys of retired people whizzed past, headed for a nearby scenic overlook, and the locals buzzed home for their weekends. The weekend rush hour started earlier than I had ever suspected: traffic sounds diverted our attention from our books around the noon hour! This year seemed the worst ever; additional truck-engine noises and back-up warning beeps in the valley continued during all of our visits. They had to be building an enormous house down there, but the hedge dividing Mr. Penney's original farm shielded the construction from our curiosity.

Years ago, it was so quiet that we were almost spooked by the stillness, especially at night. The valley clung to the noise of a lone car as its engine droned, mile after mile, approaching from the west. The sound got louder until headlights finally flashed past the house, and both sound and noise disappeared over the hill and faded into the dark. Flatlander families, such as ours, headed to their summer 'camps' on Friday nights. Long after we'd arrived and settled down to sleep, automobiles continued to fly past, the Penney's house temporarily blocking their reverberation. The racing stream dwindled for the remainder of the weekend, that is, until Sunday afternoon, when everyone began to hurry home.

Once, Aunts Betty and Dottie drove up to Wellsboro for a few days, bringing my cousin with them. After lunch and a grand tour of the place, Dad spent his afternoon repairing an old lawn mower, while under a cloudless sky, the rest of us sauntered across fields. The aunts told stories and laughed at their own jokes. My brother and cousin ran ahead then raced back breathlessly, claiming they had seen "the ol' bar." From their ill-disguised mimicking of Mr. Penney's pronunciation, I thought it must be a lie, but still—could it be true? Aunt Betty waved them away with a disdainful snort, and they turned around and ran back to the woods.

"A clear indication," Aunt Dottie remarked, giving me a side-long look, "that there is no such bear."

Deep in the woods, hidden under a clump of hemlock trees, water seeped from the rocks of a little spring in the hillside. Amid the stealthy mosquitoes, we dipped our hands into the cold water and slurped, interrupting the serenity of the scene. Mom and Natalie expanded the tiny clear pool by rearranging the surrounding rocks. The water momentarily clouded, and the rest of us busied ourselves by constructing rock steps that led to the spring. As we searched the woods for flat stones farther up the hillside, we ran over little mounds beneath the towering white pines. They were fun to race up and over, but what were they? Aunt Betty suggested that they were Indian burial grounds. My eyes widened.

"You must pay homage to the Indians before stepping over them," she added solemnly. I had a queasy but curious feeling in my stomach. Dead Indians? Aunt Betty paused at the base of one little hill.

"ARR-rahh-RAH-RAH. ASSSIAMO-BU-BON-no," she chanted. Then she glanced sideways at me and burst into a merry peal. I giggled happily. Aunt Betty always made things fun.

We fashioned a wobbly railing alongside the steps by resting a beech limb on two 'Y' shaped crooks of thick sticks pushed deeply into the soft earth. Aunt Dottie jauntily stuck the white bone of an old deer skull onto the lowest crook. "To ward off evil spirits," she winked. I stared, wondering if she meant it. Our walk back across the sunny fields revealed no sign of dead Indian spirits or bears—although the boys were still shouting their warnings.

Dinner was lively and when darkness settled, it found us lounging in aluminum folding chairs or lying on the wooden porch boards. We gazed at the stars and, while we all listened, Aunt Betty entertained my dad with a story. Mom asserted that Aunt Betty always exaggerated, and that every time she told the story she remembered the details differently.

"How could you remember anything?" Aunt Dottie interjected. "You were always sick, getting Mother to baby you." Aunt Dottie added that she, herself, didn't remember the story at all; then Aunt Betty silently threw her head back and shook with mirth. She turned my cousin in the direction of the car and directed him to fetch some fireworks.

Now, fireworks were illegal in Pennsylvania, though everyone had access to sparklers and little smoking balls. Aunt Betty, however, had acquired more momentous explosives—probably by crossing the Maryland border on one of her many excursions—and soon the rockets and flaring lights lit up the lawn. For the final hurrah, we trudged across the dew-damp grass to light "The Screamer," as it was henceforth dubbed, on the road.

"Five dollars is an unbelievable sum to waste on a firecracker," my mom remarked, but with Aunt Betty, extravagance for unnecessary entertainment was to be expected. In the quiet blackness, Mark lit the top of the cone and then leaped back onto the embankment.

An ear-piercing shriek emanated and my heart pounded at that shrill, inhuman sound, layered on the surrounding quiet. I imagined distant neighbors cowering in their beds. When the noise finally faded, the ensuing stillness hovered and finally sank into my shaking frame.

The voices of motors, construction and my children are all searing into my soul these days, rendering me slightly disoriented and as weary as Matthew was today. I left home in quest of the peace and quiet I have experienced here in an era past, but all in vain. The distractions of my life follow me.

Stream of Projects

Spend all you have for loveliness,
Buy it and never count the cost …

—Sara Teasdale, "Barter"

The farm was a five-hour car drive away from home. The big Penney house, purchased from their estate by my parents, had sat empty for years and was in need of extensive work. Its restoration was halted by my father's illness and I never will know his exact plans for it. He simply liked to fix things, and the farm provided an endless stream of projects. His hammer, which I have saved, has a smoothness of handle caused by frequent use. I remember, one time, standing in the glaring morning sun when Dad allowed us to help him to mix mortar. His long fingers curved around the handle of a pointed trowel as he deftly spread the thick gray cement. A flicker of a memory of a poem—something about the tools becoming an extension of work-roughened hands—teases me, reminding me vividly of my father.

A year after Dad's death, I turned a deaf ear to all reasonable objections to purchasing this land. Every time my husband lamented the ridiculousness of buying a "second home before the first," I would quote Mark Twain: "They aren't making any more land." The memories and my need to feel attached to them and the land were stronger than practical considerations.

Thus, the farm continued to be our summer camp. The

best word for the big house was—and still is—'dilapidated': jagged glass adorns the windows, and paint peels from the wooden siding. The little house was deteriorating, too, from lack of care. We spent many weekends mowing the lawn and frantically repairing breaking windows.

Living two hundred miles away and busy with our careers, we began to realize that the place was something of a burden. We spent many weekends mowing the lawn and frantically repairing breaking windows. Still, it was a retreat where I could garden and wander the fields, and Tom could relax as he golfed nearby. Most of all, Dad's presence seemed to be there. One autumn, while I was ostensibly writing my PhD thesis, we re-shingled the roof by ourselves, a repeat of the project my siblings and I had tackled with Dad twenty-five years earlier—a testament to the power of confidence established by undertaking ambitious tasks in childhood.

After my own children were born, my free time was even more limited than when I had a career, so our slap-bang fixes were fewer and the houses fell further into disrepair. As my father's daughter, I found and still find these projects to be enjoyable challenges. My husband most assuredly does not. Tom's parents pay for even the simplest home repairs, and he is uncomfortable attempting unfamiliar projects. It is still a challenge to convince him that we can fix something ourselves, and then an even bigger challenge to actually fix it.

Tom would argue that his free time was finite, and he didn't want to waste it learning to install a water pump; he would rather golf. I slowly realized that his argument had value. I wanted to be in my vegetable garden, planting herbs or picking blueberries, more than I desired to attempt to fix a frayed electrical wire. The little house was beyond our bandaging; the need for some major renovation was discovered at nearly every visit. So we increased the planting and gardening work but delegated the heavy construction to outsiders. After dealing with shoddy work done by poor carpenters, we hired an excellent craftsman and spent two years watching the little house undergo a miraculous transformation.

Linoleum was stripped from the floors to reveal their original wide planks, a new hand-hewn beam porch and new siding were added. Upstairs one bedroom was converted to a bathroom and an addition over the kitchen provided space for a new second bedroom. We still marveled that we had "bought our second home before we even had the first," but, despite the cost of the renovations, we were pleased with the results. Our sons would learn how to watch the clouds for weather conditions, plant potatoes and sunflowers, and catch the descendants of the 'hoppy' toads Mr. Penney had shown us. The little house, no longer sporting that asphalt siding that had so rankled my sensibilities, was pleasing to our eyes, both inside and out.

My dad would have approved.

What Dream, Next?

Life never leaves you with your conquests,
does it?

—Anne Morrow Lindbergh, The Flower
and The Nettle

I love being at home with my sons, watching them grow and being a part of their lives. I see myself in seven-year-old Matthew—his joy of discovery, his quiet reflective side, his imagination. Baby Michael is not a baby anymore, but a chubby being full of gurgling happiness. We live amid a forest of towering hemlocks, with a pasture in front and beautiful views of the mountains across the creek, in the northeastern corner of Pennsylvania. The boys turn over rocks to look for salamanders and my husband has a challenging but well-paying job.

Three years ago, Tom sold his accounting practice in New Jersey to take a permanent job as a chief financial officer. We relocated and rented a lovely house in a year-round lake community in the Pocono Mountains, a hundred miles closer to Wellsboro. Now that we could visit the farm without sacrificing an entire day in transit, our visits were becoming more frequent.

He belongs to the golf course of his dreams. I'm home now—with a relaxed schedule and few demands from the outside world. My back, injured years before, is healing, thanks to regular exercise.

In many ways my life is idyllic. Yet, somehow, despite all this, two healthy children and a nice husband, I am not completely satisfied. I somehow lack a creative outlet. I had been considering, lately, that all my scientific learning, which I spent years acquiring, is locked inside me with no outlet.

I worked hard for my degrees in the fields of chemistry and pharmaceutical chemistry and then in human exposure assessment—a program that linked medical issues and environmental science. I studied the effects of pollution—everything from lead paint to pesticides, indoor air quality to tropospheric ozone—on humans. I, along with more talented colleagues, spent years teasing out scientific details that were entangled in complex and complicated systems. It was fascinating and challenging and ever-changing. I liken it to making discoveries at the end of the universe while everyone else was staring no farther than the moon.

Now at home with the children, I miss being on the cutting edge and knowing the latest discoveries first-hand. No longer in the research world, I feel somehow trapped. All my knowledge is bottled up inside my small body, unavailable for dissemination, and therefore useless and unappreciated.

Saturday, August 23, 2008

The boys and I spent the hot day picking blackberries and staying on the hammock in the shade, playing 'Coast Guard rescue,' a simple game concocted by Matthew. He insisted that we all repeat the drama over and over, to his satisfaction, jumping onto the hammock, yelling the commands. At times I could hardly conceal my boredom, although I adore his earnestness and enthusiasm. I cannot decide if I am resolutely encouraging imagination or merely too spineless to curb my children. I fear the latter, but was too exhausted to stop him. Alone for four days with the boys, I felt dull-witted and despondent.

I expected that Tom would arrive to spend the afternoon and stay the night, but the day dragged on with no sight of him. We wandered up to the barn, poked around through the piles of dusty old things, then climbed onto the hay rolls that dot the field on the hill. Finally, wearily, I realized that Tom had to work all day after all and wouldn't be coming. I left the boys to push toy trucks in the stone trench alongside the house while inside I stared absently into the refrigerator, trying to plan dinner.

Car tires crunched the gravel on the driveway. Tom was here! I shut the refrigerator door and hurried after the boys, who had deserted the trucks to run to him pell-mell. I lifted one eyebrow as I noticed his long, plaid shorts: he had said that he would be working all day. He greeted us with large and enthusiastic hugs, glowing with good-will and red-faced with sunburn.

"I played eighteen, which is why I didn't get here 'til now," he admitted, as he left the boys to their trucks and followed me into the house to help with dinner and catch up on the news. His freedom to decide to do something fun without making extensive babysitting arrangements vaguely annoys me, especially today, because he ostensibly stayed home to work. However, I was too tired and hungry to start an argument.

It was good to see him. After we'd eaten and the dishes were washed, he began playfully wrestling with the boys on the living room floor. Their excitement soon escalated into a raucous, tumbling affair as I pleaded for them to stop, to be just a little quieter; my head ached. Realizing the futility of my requests, I grabbed the lone piece of mail addressed to me that Tom had brought from home. I plopped into the wooden rocker on the front porch, took a deep breath and sighed.

Peacefully still, I was alone for the first time in four days;

no one demanded my attention. True, Tom was leaving tomorrow, but he would be back on Wednesday, so we could spend the Labor Day vacation together. I had longed to spend such an extended visit here, and now it was happening, though it was slightly more exhausting than anticipated.

I watched the sky's peach-tipped clouds as I gently rocked the snarls out of my soul. Into my mind flitted an advertisement from the latest journal of a distinguished publication. I had scanned it briefly, last week, but hadn't had a moment to contemplate the possibility:

> The Pennsylvania State University, College of Medicine, Department of Public Health, seeks a tenure-track Assistant Professor to expand its epidemiology research program in the area of Environmental Health ... Priority is given to applicants with strong experience in Environmental Exposure Assessment ...

My brow had furrowed as I considered the possibility: "Why, my degree is in that very field!"

It was a position in a small Pennsylvania city; the job would be reasonably close to our families and to this farm. The science would be easy to grasp and interesting, although I might have to establish a lab. I ruefully recognized that I lack the patience and likely the skill to maintain state-of-the-art equipment. Still, I had been considering applying for the position. They were searching for a scientist with experience right up my alley!

In this free moment alone, I mulled over the possibility of a job interview.

Well, I would have to generate an extensive formal presentation on my thesis topic, which was now—what?—

nearly ten years old. I would have to read the current literature to be prepared to discuss new research on that subject … Oh, and any recent 'hot' subjects in the field, too. I would have to skim the journals published over the past year. I would have to be abreast of the research that the Penn State faculty was currently performing and generate a strong idea for my own future research plan.

Oh, and funding sources … I would need to compile a list of potential funding sources. *Good luck with that one.* I sat, dully, now transfixed not by the beauty of the scene, but by the enormity of the challenge.

When on earth will I find time to do even the first of those?

I shook my head slowly. I never seem to sit down, except for a few minutes at the end of the day when I collapse on the couch and stare at the walls before finding one last chore that needs to be done before bed. True, I cannot pinpoint just what I do with my days, but then, what woman, staying home all day with a toddler, is able to point to anything tangible? Everything I do is repetitive—feeding and washing little mouths, diaper changing, laundry, cleaning—and it needs to be done today, tomorrow, and every day after that.

I think of something a woman in a quilt shop once said to me: "When my kids were little, the quilting I did at night was the only thing I did that stayed done." Now I understand what she meant.

Nothing stays done in my parenting job, I thought, rocking the chair faster.

My present life is not structured to allow me to be successful as a university faculty member, not even, it seems, to interview for the position. I spend my days at home with finger paints and mud pies.

"When would I even find time to locate an outfit for the interview?" I murmured. The one suit I still have hangs in the back of Matthew's closet, behind his stuffed animals. It is a relic of those scientific days, of the cutting edge research I presented here and in Europe. I am not sure why I keep the suit, except as a reminder that I once lived a different life.

I imagined trying to grab a few minutes with the boys while slapping pans around the kitchen—still wearing that suit—after a harried commute in the rain. I could not do it well enough, and, truthfully, I do not want the associated stress.

I do not want to be a professor, now, at this stage of my life. I would hate being trapped in an office on the sixth floor of some city building, frantically juggling five grant proposals and dealing with all the faculty politics, fixing laboratory equipment and struggling with demands from all angles. I have watched skilled researchers founder under the pressures of seventy-hour work weeks, hoping to be considered for tenure.

But, if a faculty position was written for me, this would be the one.

I sighed again.

"What I really want," I mused, staring at the sky, "is to write. I want to write!"

I have wanted to write since childhood, but not to make up stories. "I want to write about Wellsboro, to capture and lock all those memories of this place and of my dad onto paper, for myself and for my children."

I said it aloud.

Derrick

And all the Noise, Noise, Noise … how I
hate all that noise!

—Dr. Seuss, The Grinch Who Stole
Christmas

My thoughts returned from gyrations about job
opportunities to notice the spectacular sunset and the
warmth of the evening. It was my favorite time of day, when
the earth seems still and peace reigns. I noticed the envelope
on my lap and opened it—a letter from Matthew's school.
Likely some fundraiser, I thought, rocking gently. Unfolding
the top page, I glanced, squinted more closely, then scrambled
out of my seat with my heart pounding.

"School starts the day after tomorrow!" I nearly shrieked.
"School starts THIS Monday, not next Tuesday!" I breathed
shallow, shallow breaths.

Somehow I had misinterpreted Matthew's school
calendar.

"I couldn't have!" My eyes seared across the white page
as I tried to understand. With a sinking heart, I found my
error. I had interpreted the 'phase-in' days to be only for new
students, when it was to be a 'phase-in' for the whole school. I
never seem to understand those private school letters; they
seem so vague, as if reminders for a routine whose pattern is
clear to everyone but me.

My heart flopped as a sudden, drastic realization chilled me.

"Why, we … we won't have this whole week here!"

We finally had the house more or less where we wanted it. It was still missing mirrors, hooks in the bathrooms, and doorknobs on the closets, but the big annoyance of repairs was finally over. The place was shaping to our dreams, and we had planned to crown the summer with an extended visit—no builders or painters in sight.

Now, we would have to abruptly change our plans. No, we could not stay, Matthew's academic record being what it is. There seems to be something amiss with his learning, though we have tried to help him. He isn't learning to read and seems stressed about school, so we would not want him to miss the transition days of school. I gulped and stumbled inside to break the news.

I bungled that; Matthew began to cry immediately. I didn't blame him, I felt like crying, too. Why couldn't I learn to break bad news in some composed, sympathetic way so that my child gulps and handles it stoically and heroically as described in all the parenting books? Why can't I get these things right, either?

Shaking my head, I pulled them all outside, away from the abandoned wrestling and from the news of the letter, and hurried them up the hill, only relaxing our speed as we rounded the barn to follow the grass path behind the copse of aspens. Trying to drive the confusion from my mind, we strolled next to the old Torpy pond on their side of the hedge, in the old driveway that used to be part of the bigger Penney farm. The new owners live in town, and had, I gathered, once contemplated retiring here. Their little house had been torn down when Matthew was a little boy, leaving the property rather desolate.

I had walked that pebbly driveway barefoot so many times as a child, really going nowhere, but dreaming and telling myself stories. I would check the mailbox several times a day, for no good reason, as mail came so infrequently. From our property the hedge hid the mountain in the west; even from this side trees have grown to cover the view. I squinted, trying to catch a glimpse of the sunset. Instead I saw a strange sight—a tall structure, lit up with amusement park lights.

I stopped in my tracks.

"What on earth?" I began, slowly. Despite leaves, I could detect that there was a red light high in the air, and columns of more lights bored into the darkening sky, from along two sides.

"A Ferris wheel?"

What could that be, here in this agricultural township? Not the county fair, not out here! I paused, confused, but with a sudden quirky insight, immediately realized that it was one of those new natural gas drilling derricks that had dominated the local news. The other oddities of the summer suddenly made sense.

"No wonder there has been so much noise all summer!" I said aloud. "They were building this, not a house!"

The day before, while resting on the porch and reading to the boys, I had observed two huge trucks with metal scaffolding moving slowly, in tandem, down the road. I couldn't imagine what they were carrying. An hour later I noticed the trucks again, bereft of the great metal structures, as they snorted diesel fumes and headed in the other direction. I hadn't the slightest idea they were transporting parts of a gas derrick.

All the traffic noise, the continuous beeping of truck back-up warnings were associated with preparing a well site to drill a gas well. Though I hadn't seen more than lights in the darkness, I was certain.

We returned to the house and got the boys into bed. We shut the windows—all but a crack—to reduce the noise of now pervasive hammering on the metal derrick that reverberated from the mountains. Whirring sounds echoed as the sky darkened. Clangs on metal and the grinding of heavy machinery prevailed all night, and rumbling, as if a diesel engine was idling, ruined our sleep. I lay in the stifling hot room, listening to the droning, with a sick feeling that the time and space around this vacationland were dwindling and becoming fragmented. My son's school demands are carved into my calendar and over the years the small town's suburbs have, even here, spread toward our property.

And tonight, this very night, an awful, non-stop industrial noise is bombarding us. I thought of the stillness of the past years, knowing that even my experiences here as a child could not compare to the silence that the Penneys must have enjoyed, seventy years ago. We are decades past quiet. Trucks and cars zoom past the house, gas derricks are assembled with clangs and hammering … There goes my country retreat of peace and quiet.

The Offer

The one thing that does not abide by majority rule is a person's conscience.

—Harper Lee

The next morning I went to church to have some time alone. Town was quiet and the church on the corner moderately attended, but after I shook hands with the minister and exited, I left only marginally at peace. As I was leaving town, I had a strange compulsion to see the gas derrick, the same feeling I have when I pass a car crash: I must see how awful it is.

Turning onto the road nearest to where I had seen the drilling rig lights, I immediately noticed a new driveway in a fallow field. About five hundred feet back from the road, the gravel led to a leveled area and small, new buildings dominated the scene.

I stopped the car at the edge of the road and scanned the construction mess. Trucks were everywhere and large metal tanks were strewn in a seemingly haphazard fashion. Three-foot high black canvas roped off a large area—some sort of holding pond, I supposed. Two men in hardhats were conversing amid the noise, their arms gesturing at various objects.

Ah, I was right, I thought, it is a derrick! There it is, off to one side of the buildings. The trailer had to be headquarters for the project.

The noise was much louder here than at home. This awful racket had to be terrible for the people along the road. *Imagine this in MY field all summer. What a mess. I will never allow an industrial site on my land! Never!* I started the engine and shifted the car into gear. With a sick and solemn heart, I drove home to find the boys.

There is a general assumption, I gather, from Tom's summary of the local golf course gossip, that gas drilling is a good thing for the whole community. After they leave in six months, they restore your land—or so I have heard. But has something irreparable been damaged in the process?

As I pulled into my driveway, I mumbled to myself, "There is no acknowledgment, I guess, that there could be negatives from drilling, or that we shouldn't even be burning fossil fuels. Can the shale sustain the fracturing? The dollar offerings are making people jump, without any consideration of the environmental impact or the health impacts from noise and air pollution."

How often I had struggled with that concept, trying to reach people from a level of scientific expertise, people who were not ready to hear the message. I felt helpless to change things then and I couldn't overcome my dismal outlook now. Here was a big, loud industrial mess in my vacation spot, and I had no means to stop it.

৵৵৵৵

The other events of the day are vague in my mind. Tom packed his bags. *He is always in a hurry to leave*, I thought sadly. He left early so he could be home to go to work the next day and probably get in a few holes of golf before dark. He would call the principal and explain our mix-up.

Now I was discouraged for many reasons: the gas drilling, the end of summer, Tom's desire to leave early. I feel such an emptiness when he leaves. I know I should be independent, but after he is gone I feel I have lost something—a happy piece of my life. I rallied to play with the boys and pick berries for the rest of the lonely afternoon.

Late that night Tom called, and as the little emergency cell phone rang, I pushed buttons frantically, until I finally heard his, "Hello? Hello?" on the other end.

"Hi." I answered breathlessly.

He had had a long drive home. "There was a big truck accident. Can you believe it, up there, in the middle of nowhere? So I didn't golf."

I expressed sincere sympathy for the former and was secretly happy about the latter. He had talked to the principal and arranged for Matthew to begin school on Tuesday. Well, that was a relief; Tom had handled it so I didn't have to. I sometimes need a break from the management of all aspects of the children's lives.

I stood by the window to get better reception and Tom paused, before clearing his throat. I could tell he had something he wanted to discuss—something more important than the school issue, something that was preying on his mind. He was cautiously marshalling his thoughts, I could tell. Vaguely, I wondered if he was in love with another woman and had decided to leave me. In gardening jeans, with soil-roughened hands and wildly mussed hair, I certainly wasn't the well-groomed country club wife. Even when we were dating, I didn't quite fit the golf scene. I once had used a nine iron to remove some tent caterpillars from an overhanging tree on the 12th hole.

"What are you doing!?" he had expostulated with shock. I had stared back at him in equal amazement. Wasn't it obvious?

"A cherry tree would be decimated by those caterpillars! They love cherry leaves, but destroying the nest might prevent complete damage to the tree."

We laughed about it, and about our different dreams: his

was to golf at his country club near a nice suburb; mine was to grow all our own food on our own homestead. Otherwise, we had seemed so well matched.

He had been caught up in work issues for months now, and we really hadn't been that close, lately. The boys were always demanding our attention, interrupting any conversation we started. I find that especially annoying at dinner. All day, I have no adult time. I sighed as I thought of it. Well, anyway, so much of our talk was about plans and the logistics of those plans:

"What time did you schedule your exercise class?"

"What do you want to do for dinner tomorrow?"

"Is your mother coming to visit, after all?"

What did it matter if these mundane remarks were interrupted?

Of course Tom always made a joke of it when I, in moments of insecurity, would ask, "Are you going to leave me for another woman, like Kenny* did to Louise*?" Louise was a long-time friend from junior high school.

"No, do you think I would make the same mistake? I've learned my lesson. Women take too much time away from sports." I had always given him my wryly amused look and felt reassured. I recalled now that Kenny had made flip remarks like these to Louise, as well.

Tom takes a lot of calls from those billing clerks. He interacts with many people, daily, working for a medical practice, so calls from women are normal. I had noticed, though, that after coming home from business lunches with those billing clerks, he would always make teasing comments:

"Jackie and Colleen think you have it made," or, "They think I'm a catch." I would raise my eyebrows at that. Being a scientist, I had more male colleagues than female, but the comments of *his* female friends were starting to raise my apprehension. Were these lonely women chasing him?

It wasn't the billing clerks. Tom cleared his throat again

and, using the carefully controlled voice he reserved for his especially difficult clients, delicately explained that a letter had arrived from a natural gas company. He explained that the firm wanted to lease our land for five years, for the sum of $130,000, as a 'signing bonus,' to potentially drill deep down in the shale, five thousand feet below.

All summer and even earlier that day, while staring at the drilling site, I had made a theoretical decision. Tonight the reality of the conflict hit me. I suddenly spat venom: "I don't want the land damaged. I don't want a mess on my land! I didn't buy the land to make money from an industrial venture. Forget it!" My voice became shriller. "This whole weekend has been a noisy flop. We had to readjust our vacation, and now this!"

Tom, still using his quiet 'difficult client' voice, was less emotional. "Listen, it could take a lot of pressure off of my back. Maybe I could even retire early, if the money is invested properly." Tom, the tax accountant, frets about everybody's money.

"The doctors I work for are not listening to me," he says over and over. "They do not realize that, as owners, the business comes first; they won't cut their own salaries to keep it healthy." Some of the worry spilled over to our own finances, though they really didn't need to. His paycheck was deposited directly in the bank. We have padded our bank accounts, not only because we think it the responsible thing to do, but also because we do not live extravagantly. We drive old cars, rarely shop and have no debt.

Tom mentioned that his job was in jeopardy. The rest of upper management had been fired, and he, Tom, was next on the list. I did not doubt it. We had been watching the office storm brew for many months. Way back in February, we crunched across the snowy pasture one sunny afternoon, and had outlined all the possibilities for our future if his job disappeared. I had jotted notes on a little pad of paper, holding a pencil awkwardly in my cold fingers, and stumbling while I listed the answers to the questions:

Where were the job opportunities for both of us?

Where could we live?

Where did we want to live?

After making the list with all of the options, I had felt better, though we came to no conclusions. The notepad sits in a drawer, a reservoir of written choices and ideas, should we need it.

I could agree with him, in theory, today, about the money. I had convinced him to purchase this land from my mother. It required huge renovation expenses as well as taxes, yet it provided no income. I wasn't working for a salary, now, and he was.

I would love to dump a huge sum of money into his lap to make his life easier, so he could work less. But to turn my land, this land where I relax by picking wild strawberries, into an industrial site? Why, no, I could not agree to that.

"There is so little I control in this world," I told him. "I do not want my own land to be overrun with trucks and contractors who do not love it as I do. Absolutely not!"

The phone crackled, and I lost contact. I stood by the window where the air was sharply cool and sweet, reminding me of all of the other summer nights I had spent here.

The phone rang and Tom's voice hesitated on the other end. "Hello?" It was as much the question: "Will you discuss this further?" as it was a wondering if I had figured out how to work the phone. I replied with a monotone greeting and then paused. I had said it all, as far as I was concerned, and was exhausted. He could say what he wanted. I waited, listening to the sounds of the crickets outside the window and the industrial noises across the valley.

The remainder of the conversation was long and draining. Tom wants financial security, a chance to live a life not dictated by work or bosses, an opportunity to golf and exercise when he chooses. In general, I agree that he should aspire to those goals, but I am an environmental health scientist; I cannot allow gas-drilling.

"What are the ramifications of the drilling? We don't know. I won't allow it!"

Tom dropped the soothing tone. He was frustrated that I wasn't even open to examining the possibility of signing the lease. He wanted this easy cash and was convinced that I was being unreasonable.

"At least let us consult an attorney. We could talk to Owlett, to see," he begged.

I earnestly retorted, "Every time someone nags repeatedly to convince me to do something I think is wrong, I cave eventually, and then hate myself for caving. I think this is wrong. I don't want my land destroyed! I don't want to do it."

This place shields my past summers, my present summer, and all the summers I want in the future. It is a place where I garden, a place where I can connect with nature, a place that should bring peace and quiet to my soul.

It was after midnight when I finally fell into bed, wretchedly realizing that my escape-from-reality retreat was now an erupting volcano of noise, industrial machinery and marital disharmony.

Leaving

I have learned that if you must leave a
place that you have lived in and loved and
where all your yesterdays are buried deep,
leave it anyway except a slow way, leave it
the fastest way you can.

—Beryl Markham, West With the Night

I hate leaving the farm. I had no urge to transfer us to home and felt a profound irritation that this last week of summer had been stolen from me. However, once I start organizing even the smallest little thing to take home, an odd phenomenon occurs: the desolate 'time-to-leave' feeling descends and takes charge.

We did pick berries on Monday morning and watered my new ever-bearing strawberry plants that my friend, Louise, had split and given me to tuck in among the rhubarb. Michael happily helped to dump every bucket of water, but it was time to leave, and I could feel it in my bones. There was a strange silence inside, as if the house knew, as well.

It took a few hours to finish packing, as all those last minute things take longer than I project: burying the compost, packing wet kitchen towels, finding bags for the random items that seem to have no place—the water bottle, the toy plane that Michael wanted to bring home. Nothing is accomplished quickly, these days. It was after one p.m. when I finally turned off the electric main and wedged the blocks of wood in front of the screen doors.

The boys snoozed for an hour and were well behaved for the rest of the drive; then Tom helped us to unload the car, and we ate a good dinner on the porch. To maintain the peace, both of us tacitly avoided the topic of the gas derricks. I was happy to fill the sugar water jar for the bees down in their hive in the pasture, and to see my two yellow pumpkins turning orange in the little front garden bed. By late evening, we had swung on the swings at the park, played a bit of tennis, and stared at the water shimmering on the lake. I was glad to be home and didn't want to be at the camp anymore.

"What would it be like," I wondered, "If I didn't have the farm—that second life? Wouldn't life be so much simpler? Wouldn't I accomplish more things? What would it be like, to not have an attachment to my vacationland?"

Wet, Weary Weekend

The sun for sorrow will not show his head.
Go hence, to have more talk of these sad things.

—William Shakespeare, *Romeo and Juliet*

Labor Day weekend, 2008

Each morning Matthew appeared apprehensive, standing quiet and still among the noisy, bustling, jostling kids, and after school his little freckles stood out in his pale, tired face. I was glad to take him away for the weekend, back to the farm, to try to get another few days of summer.

The day, however, was cool with rain and the little house was damp when we arrived. Tom built a fire; I picked a few berries and then we all napped heavily, as one only can on gray days. We were lazy and sluggish upon waking. I could conjure no motivation to cook, so we went to town for Chinese food.

Mr. and Mrs. Al Rawson were seated at a nearby table. The Rawsons live nearby, on acres that were split away from land that had been in his family for several generations. While the boys snatched the chips from the bowl on our table, I slipped over to greet them. Al spoke of Ruth Harper, his elderly aunt, who owns the pick-your-own blueberry farm where we go to supplement our harvest.

49

Talk, though, turned to the gas-leases.

"They are a boon to the community," Al stated.

At home, that week, Tom and I had again discussed my bigger environmental picture of the gas lease: that I didn't want to promote the use of fossil fuels. I had spent five years learning some of the human health effects that result from burning carbon products, and I couldn't support the environmental damage that could result from the increase in carbon dioxide in the air. True, I was a little vague on the global warming effects and the scientific research of the past ten years. So much research had ensued while I was changing diapers and looking for frogs with the boys that I didn't have a store of facts waiting in my brain.

Tom believes that there is no such thing as global warming. Fifteen years back, we had argued heatedly about it, and the topic is one we now avoid. Our positions are entrenched and unlikely to change, and the subject is not something we discuss anymore unless we want to fight. I hate to fight and sadly remembered that in college we had talked endlessly about everything, and had seemed so similar.

Tom is also looking at the financial impacts of not taking this gas-leasing money. His job is undeniably unstable. A monetary boost would take a lot of pressure off him, and he has been on my back for months to curb our expenses, trailing after me with the credit card bill, inquiring about every purchase. He thinks we should stop eating organic food,

"It costs too much."

During one of this week's conversations, he avoided the direct gas-lease signing conflict but mentioned that the farm's taxes might someday be hard for us to pay.

"Gas under the land will raise the value of the land. If they raise the real estate assessment sky high, where will you be? You'll lose the gas and the farm. It seems stupid to me. You'll have no control of what happens to that land, then."

I have no answers other than to repeat that it is wrong

for me. I believe that I am the steward of this land I own. I feel compelled to protect these fifty acres from development and degradation, and have done so in a place where land preservation is not largely backed by community effort. Oh, people here are surrounded by beauty, they hunt on the land, and, of course, their souls are fed by the beauty of the area, consciously or not. What I fear is that they do not worry that encroachment is quietly creeping. Thirty years ago, land to the south and east was just as unspoiled. I have lived in the Philadelphia suburbs, where one housing development at a time devoured the vast rolling farms. When something is disappearing, that is when we begin to value it. I don't think the people in rural north central Pennsylvania are as worried as I am.

Of course, this is a complex issue. Building homes means jobs, and jobs are needed to feed families. So when Al Rawson made his comment, I didn't counter with an environmental argument. It seems ridiculous to ask people to abstain from easy money that is legally their own.

The Rawsons, like everyone I know, will spend some of that gas-lease money in their community, either by extra donations to the fire company, extra visits to local restaurants, or renovations to their home. I held my tongue on the subject, and instead asked about his sister-in-law's new storefront in town. When their food arrived from the kitchen, I bid them good day and returned to our table.

Tom and Matthew were examining the paper placemats, and we discovered that both Matthew and I were born in the special year, The Year of the Dragon. Tom and I, according to the Chinese litany, were incompatible, and should avoid each other. Maybe so.

After eating, we walked along the damp, lonely street

that was now devoid of the daytime bustle of people. The candy store and other businesses were closed; the only store inviting us with its bright lights was a gift shop owned by Sharon Rawson. We ventured inside, and I bought a journal. If I was not going to apply for that Penn State faculty job, I had to get started on my new writing dreams.

In front of the fire that evening, I scribbled about my childhood trips to the farm. Each little memory sparked another; there simply wasn't enough time to capture them all, or the mood of the past, or its pace. So many little insipid things—such as the fly swatters—popped to mind, and I tried to jot the hazy picture into a cohesive story. It was an unwieldy but enjoyable task.

The next morning dawned gray again, and I felt that I could not look at Michael's little pants, drooping, still soaked on the porch clothesline, without crying. A dull weekend. Where had my summer gone?

By afternoon, the drizzle gave way to gray overcast, and I pushed the stroller through the village settlement north of town. There is a farmer's market by the end of the new rail-trail, and I bought a dozen ears of sweet corn. I hadn't been especially seeking sweet corn—except that it somehow represented summer, and these two months had been so wet and un-summer-like that I wanted something to signify August.

Matthew and Tom, at the former's pestering, had meanwhile headed to a nearby bait and tackle shop. It took me a while to join them; Michael had refused to ride in the stroller and had slowed to examine each pebble he discovered along the way. In fact, Tom had bought himself a new fishing rod by the time I walked into the tackle shop. I teased Tom about the 'necessity of not purchasing extraneous things,' a quote that had flowed out of Tom's mouth and followed me around all summer. Tom smiled and told me that he and the owner were discussing gas leases. I joined in the chat for a few minutes, while chasing Michael, who was touching everything in the small store.

The tackle shop guy told us that he owns ten acres and was so sure that the gas company wouldn't drill on those acres that he signed the lease and took the cash payment.

"Did you have an attorney look at the lease?" Tom asked.

The tackle shack guy shrugged dismissively. "Eh, their attorney looked at it." I held my breath and didn't say anything. The tackle shack guy continued, "I figured that they couldn't drill on my ten acres anyway, since they cannot drill closer than five hundred feet to a building. I might as well take their money." He then made a strange assertion that the energy company could make three offers, and if you didn't take them, they could drill under you anyway.

On the drive back to the farm, with the sweet corn and the new rod in the trunk, we pondered the possibility that the energy company could have such power. It seemed improbable.

Tom said, "If it is true, then wouldn't the gas company have to have evidence that they had sent three offers? Certified mail, or something?" Both of us thought the tackle shack guy should have had his own attorney examine the contract before signing.

The sky did clear eventually and the evening was lovely. We walked over the hill to see the wild black-eyed Susans near the old stone pile, and tried to decide if the wild cherries were choke or black cherries. We found beautiful apples growing on the tree at the edge of the bottom field, and we learned from my tree book that the tree with very prickly spines jutting from its branches was a hawthorn.

That evening by the fire, we read to the boys from a book that had grown dusty on the shelves—a story I had read many years ago, as a child. It was a cozy time for all of us, drinking tea and eating snacks and finding subjects that did not divide us.

Origins of Distrust

We are living beyond our means. As a
people were have developed a lifestyle that
is draining the earth and its priceless and
irreplaceable resources without regard for
the future of our children and the people
all around the world.

—Margaret Mead

Back home after the Labor Day holiday, Tom took
Matthew to school. After starting the laundry and
washing a few breakfast dishes, I spoke to Mom on the phone.
I apologized for not calling the night before to assure her that
we were home safely, and then briefed her of the gas-lease
situation. We had received an offer, and of course Tom
wanted to take the money.

She replied, distinctly and firmly, "Your dad and Mr.
Penney never thought that it was a good idea to lease it for
mineral rights and I am sure they were correct."

I told her that I agreed. Mom and Dad had had the few
acres of woods timbered, years ago, to help pay for the land.
The pristine white pines—whose needle carpets muffled
sounds as we walked under the towering trunks, and where
Aunt Betty had warned of Indian curses—had been
destroyed. We were sickened at the sight of mess of scattered
trees and limbs and truck tire ruts gouging the hillside.

"It will take thirty years to recover," my mother had

lamented. "The logging company said they would only take a few of the biggest trees. They took so many more and left a mess. We will never again allow logging on the land."

The years went by and we didn't even try to enter the devastated woods; there was no way to walk easily through the jungle of piled-up branches. A neighbor offered to clear some for firewood, and Dad bartered for a stack for our small woodstove, but the woods were never the same. Later, brambles covered the forest floor; then small trees grew in the deep gullies that now cut through the hillside. The forest is somewhat restored, with small maples and beech trees, but the awe-inspiring pines and hemlocks are gone for good. We wouldn't be duped again, not if I had a say in it.

With a sick feeling in the pit of my stomach, I told Mom the dollar amount for the gas lease. After a moment's pause, she said in a small voice, "Well, it might be worthwhile for that amount."

I resented an opinion reversal influenced by money, and certainly one formed at that speed. Now petulant, I said, "I don't think it is right to promote the burning of fossil fuels."

I am not one who argues well, or even entirely coherently. My brain cannot think fast enough to convert new ideas into smooth verbal displays of intelligence. Usually I simply dismiss any urge to convert others. Today, however, was an exception as I added, "Someone has to stand up for their beliefs and put their money where their mouth is. I have decided to be that one."

Mom did not try to convince me but shifted to the topic of no contention, namely the kids, but the conversation was forced. When I hung up the phone, I wondered if I would allow my resolve to be sanded into oblivion. I sat on the small stool in the kitchen and took a deep breath.

I hoped I could live up to my statements and ideals.

When Tom called from work later, I mentioned the conversation with my mother, how I had been reminded of the deception my parents had experienced when they allowed their timber to be cut.

"These companies don't care about the land; they just want to take one resource, as quickly as possible, without regard for the damage left behind." I reminded him of the ruts in the woods that caused erosion, scars that still have not healed on our land. But, now cued by the subject of timber, not the land damage, Tom asked me to consider natural gas as a resource, like wood or hay. I hastily brushed that argument aside, replying that it is not renewable, that I knew better than to promote it, even if the world didn't. Besides, what I feared was that there would be other, as yet unforeseen, ramifications.

Tom was beginning to be agitated by my refusal to consider this opportunity to make easy cash. "It is lying on the ground, waiting for us to pick it up," were his words. The futility of his attempts to dissuade me from my stance was starting to abrade his calm demeanor. He was clearly provoked, and having dug my heels into my position, I was watching the companionship of our marriage erode. A coolness had settled between us, a thin icy barrier that chilled our friendship and couldn't be ignored.

My lack of articulateness was one source of confusion. I had never expressed my desire to protect the land from development. But why would he think otherwise? He knew that I had never viewed the land as a real estate development site.

I only knew that I didn't want someone with heavy machinery ripping my fields to shreds, building roads and damaging the scene. Plus, there was a bigger world issue: burning fossil fuels is a bad idea, and who knows what else is released into the air during the drilling process? The result might be many adverse health effects.

"Why would I get a PhD in Environmental Science if I was willing to let the land be destroyed?" I asked.

To that, Tom called me a hypocrite. "You don't really believe that burning fossil fuels is bad, or you wouldn't use them yourself." His comment silenced me, and with this advantage, he continued, "You say you care about the environment, but that is not true. If you really cared about the environment, you would give up your car and live in the city."

He had said as much many times, and the comment always stung. How could I respond? His point cannot be denied: if I lived in the city, I would be less likely to use a car. But would I use less energy? I am not sure. I could not plant such a big garden, or hang my laundry outside on the line. My entertainment would likely be 'artificially generated,' and that would cost energy. We had tried city life, and I detested the closed-in feeling of having too many people and houses and too few trees and plants in my world.

City life, to me, is contrived. Once there, I forget the nuances of nature and I am apt to be less aware of the abundance of non-recyclable as well as the 'not recycled' garbage than when I am in the woods. In the city, surrounded by the unnatural, my mind does not consider the natural. At home, in the country, I notice even one piece of non-degrading plastic, and it seems remarkably out of place. Here in the woods, I consider how rash, extravagant purchases of unnecessary items are taking a toll on our natural resources, and it reminds me to think before I buy.

There are benefits to living in an urban community, I realize. Grocery stores stock the piles of organic foods and specialty breads where I happily plunge my greedy little fingers, but I would rather live in a rural area.

Later in the evening I sat, deep in thought, while the boys hit golf balls on the front lawn. How could I stop using fossil fuels completely? People lived without fossil fuels and had done so for thousands of years. The Amish still do without them, so why couldn't I? Is it just that I am lazy?

I considered what it would take for me to stop using the

fuels. For one, I would have to grow all our own food and store it for the winter. How could I grow our own food, cook it over a wood fire, and save enough to eat during the winter? How many berries could we harvest?

And what about, I gasped, our CLOTHING?! It suddenly dawned on me that we would have to get all our clothing from sheep wool, or deerskins, or plants. What a thought! How on earth could I make all our own clothes?

"It would be a radically different existence," I murmured, then added, "What an understatement!"

I stared at the little boys playing on a lawn that had nourished horses for so many years. Landlords notoriously do not like land disrupted by transient families. If we owned this rental home, I would convert the pasture to a big garden.

"Even so, a garden wouldn't be enough. We would want chickens, for their eggs and meat." I stopped my whispered musings, paling at the thought. I have seen chickens flapping around after their heads were chopped off. It was a bloody mess. I am happy to leave butchering to others.

My thoughts returned to the less controversial subject of clothing.

"Well, we would need sheep for wool … and they would have to be sheared and the wool washed, dried, carded, spun, and woven. Why, that's a full-time job! When would I have time to cook our meals, do laundry, or harvest the garden? My mind reeled as I realized how free my life is, simply because I do not need to make any of my own clothing.

"If I had to do it all myself, I'd never have a moment of ease to read or relax!"

Later, when Michael and Matthew were splashing in the tub, I knelt beside it and washed Michael's soft skin. He kicked the water and chattered incessantly as Matthew filled the tub with more and more warm water. My thoughts slid back to the self-sufficient natural life. I wouldn't be able to use metal pipes, so hot water would be out of the question … not a pleasant thought. I opened the cabinet and pulled a soft white towel. I didn't think cotton grew here, but I'd heard they could make fibers from the inside of stinging nettles and flax plants. Where would I get a soft towel?

In our current family unit and cultural structure, is self-sufficiency even conceivable? Is it desirable? I want to live simply, but I also want the conveniences of my modern lifestyle. Unfortunately, the latter are powered by fossil-fuels.

Gut Feelings

"You can put your socks in the oven, but that don't make them biscuits."

—Gladiola Montana, Never Ask A Man the Size of His Spread

One evening the next week, Tom reiterated his concern about the tackle shack guy's comment:

"Do you think it is true that if they send you three offers and you refuse, they can drill anyway? If they are going to drill anyway, we might as well take some money for it."

"How can they possibly be allowed to drill on our land?" I insisted. "It makes no sense. This is America, not some communist country!"

Indeed it didn't make sense to us, and we hadn't put much stock in the assertion, but it was worth getting the facts. So, to appease Tom and address this barrier in our marriage, I agreed to speak to an attorney about the gas lease. Yet I was thinking, miserably, of the time I had been yanked into a discussion about a position I didn't want to alter and then caved.

જાજાજાજ

I had been a part-time faculty member, teaching nursing chemistry to community college students near Pittsburgh. One student—far older than I—had failed to do even the modest amount of make-up work required for a passing grade and so had failed the class.

It was a pity that she was taking Chemistry at all, because General Chemistry involves extensive calculations that demand a strong math foundation to complete, and she had taken only the brief six-week course in algebra. Six week intensive courses are not appropriate for all subjects. Not only did she not grasp algebra, she also appeared to be missing another prerequisite for my class. Though her attendance in my class was reasonable, I simply could not pass her.

I asked the dean why this student had been able to continue to this point. "Why was she allowed to advance without the requirements that would establish a foundation for future success? No wonder she failed my class."

"Our prerequisites are not required," the dean informed me with a serious face. I was dumbfounded. Prerequisite means 'required to have taken previously.' Astonished, I wondered, but didn't ask, the obvious question: Why not?

It is a vague memory now, but the dean and I painstakingly went over every error in each of her exams with her. We explained that the grade could not be changed. I had thought the matter was closed.

"Even with a calculator," I explained, as nicely as possible, "part of your trouble is that you needed to have a stronger background in Algebra, in order to know which math manipulations are needed for the Chemistry calculations." The dean agreed; the matter was closed.

Yet this student, who either lacked the drive or mental training to learn the material, persisted in her campaign to get the grade changed. The college staff met one evening to discuss the situation, because she evidently was causing a furor. The president of the college was, I discovered, the attractive woman cracking her chewing gum and holding a bag of potato chips, at the far end of the table. The various deans were there, all looking old and weary, and we got down to business.

The nursing teachers insisted that this student needed to become a nurse so she could support her husband and children. They clearly believed me to be bent on impeding the student's progress. They implored me, with choking voices, to change her grade. I was baffled that anyone would want or expect me to act dishonestly. It would be unfair to me, to her, and to her classmates—not to mention the patients who she might eventually harm. "I was assessing her ability to understand Chemistry. That was my job." The simplicity of my reply silenced them.

We went on to review, again, all of the student's work, as they critically eyed every answer on each page. My paperwork, however, was in order and my records were complete; the college agreed to uphold my decision. The nursing teachers glared at me as I left. I hated this mess, but as far as I was concerned, it was over.

I wished. Somehow someone must have bungled something on the official end, because within a month, the nightmare resurfaced. The student had hired an attorney, one who was noted in the local education community for disputing policies. My hands were clammy as everyone reassembled in the room, this time with the student and her attorney present. Today, the memory of her lawyer's interrogation is still with me, though I refuted every question he politely posed, and he listened respectfully. The staff sat silently, listening to the repartee. At the end, the lawyer addressed the president of the college—who had opted not to chew gum or eat chips on the occasion—and concluded that there was nothing that Mrs. Hamel had done that seemed unreasonable. My leg, which had been twitching under the table, stopped shaking.

It was then that the college president asked the student and her lawyer to leave for a moment. I couldn't think of a reason for this request, and I glanced triumphantly at the student as she skulked out of the room. I took a deep breath and released it. I had an itchy feeling that I, too, should fold up my papers, button my suit coat and leave. I rose to leave, but the dean leaned over and put her hand on my arm.

"Please stay, Stephanie, a few moments." I sat.

The president asked me if I would consider allowing the student to complete the work that she hadn't finished. I was momentarily surprised that none of us had thought of this compromise earlier.

"Well, of course, why not?" I agreed. It would be a win-win situation. She could learn the material, and the matter would be dropped for the school. The whole roomful of people seemed to let out a collective breath. Again, I stood to leave.

In hindsight, I should have bolted. Being young, I did not, since the dean again put her hand on my arm, this time saying, sweetly, "Stephanie, it would save a lot of time if you could sign the grade card now. We won't have to mail it back and forth, and since you commute such a long distance, you won't have to drive it back. I will keep it, signed, on my desk, until the work is completed to your satisfaction."

I looked at her suspiciously. She smiled blandly into my face.

"I must be paranoid," I murmured to myself, agreeing to sign. The other dean and the university officials relaxed in their chairs, again, and struck up small talk as she hurried away to fetch the card.

I was naïve; I trusted, and so I signed the card. However, paranoia assailed me again as I sat for a moment. The dean leaned over, still purring, and recommended that I head home, since, "We know you have such a long drive, dear." I stood up and, though everyone smiled at me, a strong impulse surged inside of me. I almost—almost—reached across the dean, snatched the card, and ripped it up. I didn't, however, and to this day I wish I had.

If I had followed my gut feeling, I might have received

make-up homework from that student who wanted her grade changed. The matter might have concluded with the staff of the college taking responsibility for bungling some protocol. Instead, I never saw any material from the student, and I later heard rumors that she was bragging that she had gotten the grade changed.

Nearly twenty years later, with that unrelated outrage still lurking in my memory, I feared that my fortitude would again be undermined if I met with a group of people deviously bent on manipulating me in this gas-lease situation.

"I will not go against my gut feeling again!"

Royalties

Love the time the chance unfolds before
you
Love the time it takes to find the truth
Love the time you dance with the mystery
Love the wisdom of the old and the vision
of the youth.

—David M. Bailey, "Love the Time"

In this situation, though, there was an unknown: What are they allowed to do underground?

"Maybe we can negotiate that they pay us for the gas that they take, even if we do not allow them to drill." Tom had offered.

I sighed deeply, "We can call Owlett some time. But I do not want to change my mind. My gut tells me it is the wrong thing to do."

Tom said nothing more, but the first minute he could, he called to arrange a conference call with our attorney in Wellsboro, Tom Owlett. He had prepared the legal documents when we purchased the house from my mother; his father had arranged the documents when my parents first bought the house. We are on cordial terms with Owlett, who is honest, and has the quiet reserve of an intelligent man who was raised in a small town.

Luckily for me, Michael slept snuggly on my lap during our call. Being married to an accountant, I know all about billable hours and tried to stay focused on the subject, to minimize our bill from the attorney. I jotted notes. Owlett agreed to review that lease that I had thrust into the upper reaches of the old wooden cabinet, after I had scanned it briefly, a week ago. It was stuck full of red "sign here" command stickers, and the dollar amount of our offer was in capital letters. Perhaps the energy company attorneys were hoping that no one looked past the dollar signs.

Owlett briefed us on the situation in Tioga County, from his perspective.

"The gas pocket was 8,000 to 15,000 feet deep, in the Marcellus shale." The companies have technology that is capable of drilling to the shale and then horizontally, but he didn't know which direction they were going to drill at the nearby well. A company had approached him a few years back, and, thinking that the possibility was remote, he himself had signed with them, "for a whopping," he told us with self-mockery in his voice, "five dollars an acre."

He thought that they were up to around a thousand now. We told him that we were offered twenty five hundred. He whistled, then went on to say that his current lease was one hundred thirty dollars an acre, but that he would likely get a royalty check soon.

We told him that I wouldn't allow them to drill, but wanted them to pay for the gas if they did extract it from under our property. He stated it legally, saying that we wanted 'a subsurface agreement with no surface disturbance.' That wasn't quite what I had in mind; I didn't want to give them permission but wanted compensation should they remove it. My distinction, however, seemed to be an intellectual splitting of hairs.

Owlett indicated that the Tyoga Country Club, with two hundred acres, had discussed a subsurface-only agreement, but had finally agreed on the surface lease, which allows drilling on their property. We speculated as to why, and Tom suggested that it was due to the well-known fact that the country club was in a lot of debt. Owlett agreed to look into the country club negotiations. Well, I thought, a subsurface lease would be better, especially if they were going to take the gas horizontally in any case.

"The lease is broken into three parts: the pipe, the surface lease, and the subsurface lease. If you grant them anything having to do with the pipe, you must limit what they can do." Owlett was emphatic on this point. A look at the lease agreement indicated that the gas company had offered us five dollars a foot for that use.

"Right now, the lease is written so that they can put pipes in for anything—oil, gas, water, and brine. You must be very careful to allow them to have pipes for only gas, and those only when you are joined in a pool or transported to the pool. Royalties are given for those." He sounded so matter-of-fact. There were royalties to be negotiated and a percentage of the gas money would be ours.

There was something in that word, 'royalties', that suddenly conjured the image of Arabian grandeur and unfettered wealth. The idea jutted into my mind and, distracted by it, I began to ponder a life of unlimited money. Royalties, indeed, would be wonderful for our future, and they are unpredictable, a wildcard, which makes them even more exciting. I am embarrassed to admit it, but I salivated each time he said that word.

I shook my thoughts away from royalties and, with the receiver tucked uncomfortably under my ear, began again to take notes as fast as my little fingers could write. To get back to solid, self-righteous ground, I railed against the lease document they had sent.

"All those sticky tags, 'Sign here', 'Sign here', make it so easy just to sign. And there are people—the tackle shop guy, for example—who just signed and never had an attorney look it over." I said that the one-sidedness of the agreement made me angry, that they were taking advantage of the business naiveté of people. Neither Tom nor Owlett disagreed, but, with their silence, I realized, they were playing 'boys' rules, and I, 'girls.' Boys and men, according to a book I read way before I had boys of my own, tend toward the hierarchy; if you cannot keep up, you deserve to lose. Little girls often play down to the lowest skill, helping the youngest to be part of the group. I didn't waste the ticking time on the meter of an attorney by elaborating. I let Tom ask his next question, and sat quietly, with the phone tightly grasped in my fist.

Owlett answered Tom's questions and returned to a discussion on the pipelines, which he evidently thought was important: "There is a need to have developing clauses in the lease that you and the drillers must be in consensus, that you must agree to any plans regarding roads, pipes, etc. The lease is written so it won't allow unreasonable changes."

I suspected that the gas company and I would disagree on what was 'unreasonable,' and that might be a source of conflict. I realized that they could afford to sue easier than I could, and that once they are on or under our property, we are powerless to stop them. The thought grabbed me as my eyes stared out the window at the steel blue nuthatch that was crawling down the hemlock tree outside. I was suddenly struck by the futility of our position, or impotence—should we need to defend ourselves—and the conversation buzzed past me for a moment.

Owlett continued, discussing the protocol of pooling the land; the gas company would find a spot to drill and take the 'pool' of gas from beneath the land. "The maximum pool in Pennsylvania is 640 square acres, or a mile, by statute, but the geology of the dense Marcellus shale is forcing them to drill wells that are closer together: eighty or one hundred, maybe two hundred acres." I perked up again and grabbed my pen.

That isn't a good sign, I thought. They are close at that well in the valley. I thought that our owning road frontage, combined with our thirty-five acres of open field, would be ideal for a drill site. The fact that our nearest neighbors' rights were leased to another company—one that was not currently drilling in the area—made my land seem to be even more of a prize for drilling, in my mind, at least.

"The County planners, as of now, have permitted eight sites, and three wells have been drilled. There is one on Dutch Hill Road and there is one up Heise Run Road, as well as the new one." Owlett thought that if they started to find a lot of gas, they would begin 'punching a lot of holes around here.' I thought, rather sarcastically, that they obviously were finding gas, or they wouldn't be offering us such a big lump of cash to search for the possibility of gas.

I sat silently as Owlett interpreted the language and rules for us: "If they don't start drilling or act within five years, the lease can be renegotiated."

We discussed the importance of negotiating the best lease now, because if they started working within the next five years, the contract would be viable for as long as they were drilling. The drilling, I thought grimly, could begin, at four years and 364 days. We also needed the ability to renegotiate the lease in the future if they didn't act within that period. Owlett mentioned that he knew the local guy who was the gas company representative in the area. We talked about scheduling a meeting with him. Tom suggested that, since the company might need only five acres for the well site, maybe we could walk our land with the representative. We could get a better idea of the possible impact on our lives and land, with that information. I frowned, but said nothing.

We asked about conservation easements. We do not have an easement, nor have we promised any land to be preserved in a nature trust, but I have long thought that it might be a good idea to keep the land from development. Tom is against the idea—as he confirmed by his silence over the phone. He wants total control over our assets, not to hand them over to some not-for-profit organization. However, if there *is* a conservation easement on the property that disallows surface disturbance, well, then they would have to offer a subsurface-only agreement in order to extract gas under the land.

Owlett said he would look into the subsurface-only lease. I asked about accountability: "How do we know what kind of environmental record they have, and who is monitoring the gas companies?"

"The gas companies must file reports to the DEP on the depth and the bottom hole production; that is public information. Reading their annual report is the only way of confirming what is actually coming out of the ground. You could examine that report, if you chose, but even then it would be very difficult to determine whether or not they were being honest."

Owlett went on to say that he was inclined to believe, from a public relations standpoint, that they would be honest. I tried to put forth my theory that public relations could be manipulated. I was thinking of the big billboards on the highway, 'Doing Pennsylvania a World of Good,' that I had seen recently. They were all sponsored by natural gas companies and showed pastoral images. Not one of them realistically represented the small industrial site created by each drill site. Pictures of Pennsylvania's rolling farm fields were not exactly an honest representation of the drilling that I had seen. However, this kind of talk was not resolving anything, and our meter was ticking.

Connection

How good it feels, the touch of a friend's
hand.

—Oliver Wendell Holmes

From the tone of Owlett's voice, Tom deduced that the
attorney wished he had a well on his property and was
getting some big royalties. This fact Tom mentioned to me
later, when we spoke two hours later, no longer on conference
call.

"Owlett just phoned me back," Tom said, "to tell me that
when he ran out for lunch, he saw the guy who had
negotiated the golf course lease. The gas company would not
accept just a subsurface lease, and so they had agreed to
negotiate a surface and therefore also a subsurface lease. Oh,
and they stopped drilling near us, for now."

Tom thought that maybe, due to the large parcel of land,
it would not be feasible for the gas company to extract the gas
from under the golf course via a nearby location. "Owlett
doubts we could get a subsurface-only lease. 'They have more
resources than you do,' was what he said." That sounded
ominous to me.

Owlett apparently had also spoken positively about my
character. Perhaps Tom had first disparaged my lack of
enthusiasm for the drilling, because Owlett had replied, "She
is a principled woman." Tom repeated this to me as we left

the kids with Rachel, our teenaged babysitter, to go kayaking on the local lake.

With Owlett's affirmation, Tom seemed to see my behavior in a different light. For the first time in two weeks, I felt that he and I were not at odds. I felt a huge weight lift off my chest. It was nice to hold hands again.

Money Confounds the Issue

The lust for comfort murders the passion
of the soul and walks, grinning, in the
funeral.

—Kahlil Gibran, *The Prophet*

As we kayaked across the lake, I couldn't stop worrying—
no longer about Tom and me, but rather about my own
willpower. When Owlett described the possibilities of
royalties garnered from gas drilling, I wanted that money. My
mind wandered into the fantasy of lavish wealth. I wanted
what those gas-lease royalties could bring, all the things I
didn't need but craved—comfort, ease, a future where we
could travel. And, if all those weren't shallow enough, I liked
the excellent service offered in expensive places.

I hated to believe it of myself, but it was true: the idea of
royalties made my knees sag. After weeks of inserting an
emphatic "No!" into every conversation, I suddenly tinkered
with the idea of caving in. *It would be easy money.* It was
sitting there, just waiting to be taken, and Tom's eyes were
glittering at the chance.

Suddenly I couldn't trust myself to do what I had already
decided was the 'right thing.' I started to fear that I would
capitulate, that I lacked strength to uphold my beliefs. Would
I decide that luxuries were more important than my ideals?

I recalled a vague story about a strong-willed family
character. My mother had told it. I can't recall the details …

something about Uncle Arkin standing up for a cause when no one else would. There is strength in my ancestry, which is grounded in Quaker values. Though the family has channeled away from the religious aspects, the pragmatic lifestyle of voluntary simplicity appeals to me. I needed to tap that line of Quaker values.

As we paddled back to the shore, Tom tried to elicit conversation. I was silent, not from animosity, but due to an incredible sadness welling inside. I wanted to save my land from drilling, but I also wanted that money. I shook my head. *What am I thinking? I cannot be thinking this, can I?*

I am not in the habit of hiding my thoughts and so mentioned my confusion to Tom while we ate at the pizza place up the road. We waited for a salad to arrive, and I dolefully admitted that I was enamored by the money prospect. This was a chance to leave financial worries in the dust, and I wanted that feeling. Tom's visibly perked up at the idea that I might yield.

"You know," he said, trying to sound casual, "There is a good chance that they wouldn't drill on the property; then you would be home free. The land would be untouched, and we could have that nice lump of money in the bank. We could travel to Florida this winter." I shifted my lips to the left and squinted one eye. I could tell that Tom was playing to my weakness, my wanderlust. The waitress left a plateful of white iceberg lettuce. After she turned away, I frowned and pushed it across the table toward Tom. "I'm not hungry." I sighed.

Back home, we fed leftover pizza to the boys and the sitter, then helped the boys tidy the maze of wooden trains they had constructed and began their bedtime routine. I had just hurried off to practice the piano when Jim McKenna phoned. Jim had managed a huge portion of the employees in a big area hospital before a reorganization left him bereft of a job. Afterward, he worked with Tom for two years before that management staff was cropped. Tom holds Jim in high esteem and was devastated when he was fired.

Jim had sent us an invitation to his daughter's wedding, and I thanked him for that unnecessary kindness. We knew neither the bride nor the groom.

Tom, who had gone to get his pitching wedge, called out: "Tell Jim how you won't let me get rich!"

"What's he complaining about, now?" Jim laughed. I mentioned our dilemma, finishing with my new openness to the idea of royalties.

Tom returned to the room and rested his club on the floor, taking the golf stance. He moaned, "Tell Jim you want me to slave away for these bickering doctors for the rest of my days, when I could be golfing." I waved at Tom to silence him, so I could hear Jim's comments. Jim didn't seem to be taking our dilemma seriously, but then, he never seemed to take anything seriously. His offhand response was, "Well, if your purpose is to save the land, you cannot sign the lease. But everyone has a price. It seems as if you have found yours."

I sadly passed the phone to Tom.

Geological Advice

It is not so much our friends' help that
helps us, as the confident knowledge that
they will help us.

—Epicurus

At spare intervals during the next few weeks, Tom and I
searched for information on the Internet and discovered
lecture notes by university faculty. We learned how the shale
fracturing process works. It seems that they drill vertically,
then cement off the drill pipe area, and add explosives to
crack the deeper shale. The explosions release gas, which is
pumped up and removed. Additional wells can be drilled
from the same site, curving to snake horizontally through the
shale layer to reach all the gas along its path.

We learned about the need for protecting the
groundwater, which might be contaminated by drilling
tailings or by chemicals, including xylenes and toluenes.
Being a chemist, I am familiar with those materials: they are
solvents, but I do not know why they are needed for the
fracturing. Questions began to formulate: Why are those
particular chemicals needed? Where do they come from?
Why do they need so much water brought in and pumped
out?" I read and wondered: Are the tailings collected? Is the
water re-collected and reused from one drill site to the next?

Given enough time, I could tackle the technical issues; it
was the legal aspect that was distressing. I uncovered the 'Law

of Capture,' apparently first written for other fossil fuels. It is a Pennsylvania legal clause stating that if minerals-(including gas, oil and coal) were captured from underneath a property belonging to someone who did not have a mineral lease, then the mineral belonged to the person capturing it. Royalties were only paid to the landowner if the neighboring mineral lease holders petitioned the company to pay royalties to the landowner without a lease. I wondered if our neighbors would willingly offer a share of their royalties to me. If I did not sign, would they forgo some profit by approaching the natural gas company to request payment to me for the portion of gas that had been captured from underneath my property?

As it seemed possible that the gas company can access our resource without our permission, Tom became agitated about my refusal to sign a lease. His patience had dwindled and our mutual goodwill deteriorated for the second time in a space of a few weeks.

When I had a few minutes, I fired off an e-mail to Frank McLaughlin. Frank is a pal who was in the Rutgers PhD program with me—a New Jersey DEP 'lifer.' His background is in hydrogeology and I'd hoped he might be able to answer questions about the natural gas drilling technology.

Frank surprised me by not giving me much new information on the geology, but instead offered a slew of newspaper articles attached to his e-mail. Apparently this topic has hit the news outside of Pennsylvania. He stays informed with the media coverage of environmental events, and I do not. I simply do not have time to sit long enough to read anything.

From: "Frank McLaughlin III"
Re: Ethical dilemma over Texas tea—Need geology advice
Stephanie:
    Your email produced laughter, tears and empathy ...

I don't envy the multi-generational decision on your hands ... Isn't it interesting that 'opportunities' have underlying curses ... This one is a doozy!

A few thoughts to assist:

First, I'm sure you know that the geological formation that the energy companies are aggressively seeking to extract natural gas is the Marcellus Shale, which extends from the Catskills south and west through PA to West Virginia and Ohio. It looks like PA may have the greatest natural gas reserves. Get to know your local geology and what the gas companies are doing in your area.

Secondly, talk to everyone about this—locals, farmers, geologists, lawyers, government officials—and hear their opinions and feelings about the many shades of this 'opportunity.'

Next, time is on your side, so don't rush into making a decision. In February, a friend of mine at the town Shade Tree Commission was offered a lease of $500/acre for his ~20 acres in Susquehanna County. This July, he was offered $2,500/acre. He owns a nursery business in NJ and he is reluctant to allow companies to soil his retreat. Interestingly, some of his neighbors are mad at the 'holdouts' because they themselves settled on ~$500/acre.

Last, and most important, this is an emotional and personal decision, so your feelings are more important than any well-thought-out logical arguments and certainly more important than money.

I'm free to listen anytime: best are afternoons from 3-5 when Frank IV and I are usually at a park. Good luck, my good friend!

—Frank

I opened the e-mail attachments and later that evening I skimmed, then printed the seven articles and took them to our bedroom. As I climbed onto the bed, Tom, who was poring over a golf magazine, glanced up from his page.

"What's it say?"

"This is big stuff," I answered dully. I had a sick feeling, realizing that the issue is even larger than I had imagined. These gas companies have seen it all before.

"We are small potatoes." It will be impossible to fight such powerful organizations. They will trample us, nodding their fake empathetic understanding, and then inevitably ruin our land … just like the smiling dean who had forced me to pass my student.

Surprisingly, my own truth was clearly stated in these articles. I had always believed that newspaper writers created dialogue, elaborated and embellished, but here it was, in print, quotations from people echoing my exact words and thoughts, such as "At first I said, 'No way,' but then I thought, 'Well, this is so much money, so I took it.' " Was I reading my own story? Was I going to relent, too, for the love of money?

Existential Moment

Human nature is not obliged to be consistent.

—L.M. Montgomery, Anne's House of Dreams

We woke to thunderstorms and heavy rain. Matthew could hardly be pulled away from the porch door and he even ventured down the two stone steps to the 'streams' that flowed beneath the gas grill under the old carport. I watched him from the doorway then looked past him at the grill.

"Oh," I murmured, dully startled, "I have a gas grill. I never thought about that." I sighed. Maybe I do have the classic symptoms of hypocrisy, just as Tom has been saying.

I had argued that I was trying not to be a hypocrite: "I attempt to minimize my impact on the environment by composting and using things for as long as I can. I do my own baking and cooking and thus try to eliminate all of the packaging garbage." I thought however, of the ice cream bars and of all of the times, with two boys hanging from the grocery cart, I had made poor environmental choices.

But the grill was supposed to be another story. When we had gotten the grill, I had congratulated myself.

"Saved something from the landfill!" I told Tom jubilantly, patting myself on the back for recycling or, in this case, free-cycling—it had come from a neighbor. I paid a few bucks at the local hardware store for a new burner and it has worked fine ever since. It's ugly but it works. I wasn't thinking of air pollution issues at the time, or of the source of the natural gas in the tank, but today, the latter consideration shocked me. Until now, I never even thought about where the gas comes from.

There is an acronym in the environmental field: NIMBY, which stands for Not-In-My-Backyard. It refers to the violent opposition that arises when something undesirable is about to invade one's territory—a landfill, for example. It is a logical and reasonable response; however, it is often accompanied by the desire to *have* a landfill for disposal, *somewhere, just not here, not in my backyard.* As I stared at the gas grill, I realized: I want to use natural gas for my grilled chicken, but I don't want to have the drilling rigs for that gas in my backyard.

The rainwater was flowing over the step in a beautiful curve, but Tom was late for work, so Matthew had to give up his vigil and be hurried off to school. After I had gotten dressed, Mike Gallo, another old pal from Rutgers University, called. As we spoke, I lounged at the dining room table with my feet on an adjacent chair; Michael played with a toy tractor.

I explained the gas-lease difficulty: I had to choose whether or not to take the money that Tom wanted so desperately. Mike replied, "Sounds like you not taking the money won't stop the machinery; it is already in place."

"I know. I know. That's the kicker. I don't think I can stop them from getting the gas and I am beginning to think that maybe I should take the money … but, *Mike*," my voice became shrill and I spoke hurriedly, "how can I, at some future date, stand up on a podium and lecture to a student audience on the adverse effects of fuel emissions on human health if I am all the while lining my own bank account with money from that very thing?!"

I took a deep breath and sputtered sarcastically, "Why, I

can just see it … some twenty-five-year-old punk will stand up and say, 'Well, Dr. Hamel, how can you stand here and tell us that this is bad, when you are leasing your land to the energy companies?'" My free arm was flailing, and I discovered that I was standing with my feet solidly on the floor. "Mike, what am I going to say? 'Well, you just don't understand: I wanted to stop them, but knew I wouldn't be able to, so I took their money like everyone else.' I am sure the inexperienced punk will be convinced by that logic!"

Mike laughed softly. "Stephanie, that inexperienced punk would be you, in the throes of an existential moment when your past self is wrestling with your more mature, worldly self. You would be that critical examiner, standing at the microphone in the audience and saying, 'It just doesn't make sense. What you are doing is not matching your statements.' "

I sighed and grinned simultaneously. Mike was right. That is exactly what I would have said. It would have seemed so black and white to a more naïve Stephanie. He encouraged me to write all these thoughts down.

"Well, Mike, I have been meaning to write some articles about my farm, but I wanted to know the ending before I wrote this story. I mean, I don't want to write about a woman who buckles and loses all self-respect. I only want to write about myself as a heroine."

"Steph, it is a story no matter what the outcome is. Start writing and don't think about the ending, yet. It's important to get all these thoughts down on paper."

He's right, I thought, after we had exchanged goodbyes. I thumped my thumb on the table, nervously. Little Michael was absorbed in attaching a spray tank to the tractor, I noted grimly.

I am too worked up about the gas-lease to write about it, I tried to convince myself. I tapped my other fingers on the table and stared through the window at the gas grill.

A sudden revelation flickered across my brain, and I sat up, suddenly at attention. Surprised, I spoke it aloud: "Why, why, saying, 'I will never…' is so easy when no one is offering you a huge sum of money to do just what you vow not to do." It is hard to forsake an offer of a hundred and thirty thousand dollars, to actually put my money where my mouth is. Truth be told, it is even excruciatingly harder to forsake a lifestyle that depends on fossil fuel.

It is very easy to have strong convictions IF no one is testing those convictions. WHAT would that punk have done? Would she have had the spine to say 'No'? Would she be a heroine if offered that much money?"

Land Value

As I drove to the car mechanic the next morning, I tried to separate the threads of the issue. I divided it all into four options:

By ignoring the lease, I could keep the gas company off of the land but not protect the gas; it could potentially be extracted. Result: No money, possible loss of gas, no land damage.

I could sign a lease and hope that they drill on another neighbor's property. In that case I could get Tom his cash, but not necessarily protect anything, land or gas.

We could try to give the land to a nature trust and stipulate that no extraction be allowed. In this instance, we'd lose a lot of control of the land, and its value as a commodity. The gas might be saved from extraction, but the land might be lost from our control. Result: Potential loss of money for boys' future, no land damage, but gas is likely protected.

The final choice is to seek a subsurface lease that would allow the company to extract the gas under my property but not have access to my land for drilling. Result: Money, no land damage, loss of gas.

The questions remain: Can they legally extract my gas without my permission, and should I take the money if I cannot protect the gas? One is a legal question, the other, an ethical one. Finally, it might even boil down to this: Which is more important, trying to save the land or trying to save the gas?

The answer, for me, personally, is to save the land from development. I know that burning fossil fuels and all of the extraction techniques are environmentally unsound and I do not want to promote it. I want to use renewable resources and less energy overall. Yet, more deeply engrained in my mind is the sick feeling I have every time I see land being converted into housing tracts or industrial parks.

During my adolescent years, countless acres of land in the Philadelphia area were transformed, as the suburbs expanded in an exponential proliferation of home building. Agricultural land typically is well-drained, or it wouldn't be used for growing crops, and combined with the attraction of being relatively uncontaminated, it is ideal land for development. Close to the city and offering safer and better schools, the suburbs exploded.

For the people whose communities were invaded, traffic became heavier, bulldozers tore through picturesque fields, and a cancer of monotype houses began to dominate the scene. I have never before tried to explain my aversion to such development, but now I know that it was because of the way it changed my community and the land. The extensiveness and indirect impacts of this invasion were mind-boggling to me. So now, if trying to compromise with my husband, I can and can protect only one—the land or the gas—I choose the land. I will always try to protect the integrity of the land.

Now the question becomes: Is it wrong to attempt to negotiate a lease for subsurface rights? We don't know the long-term ramifications of fracturing the shale, and so I still think we should not promote this endeavor.

Turtle Trouble

I speak for the trees, for the trees have no tongues.

—Dr. Seuss, *The Lorax*

Saturday, September 13, 2008.

Yesterday, I just couldn't stop being teary. Tom was going to visit his parents. The day had been wet and dreary, and when he left, the two of us glanced away from each other in chilly isolation. I do not sense that our marriage will fail; we are entrenched as partners, but this emptiness haunts me. I looked outside at the chilly rain and drooped in misery.

Today, alone with the boys, I was glad that the sun pushed through the clouds as we checked the community book shelf in the post office. I had established a free book swap in the spring, and it had proven popular. Today, the shelf was laden and some books had tumbled onto their sides. Matthew helped me stack them as Michael raced around the empty post office, hopping and yelling happily. Opening one of the empty 'package lockers' located on the opposite wall, he climbed in and hollered, "Find me!" as the door swung shut behind him. Matthew and I exchanged a glance, laughed, and pulled him out. As I returned to the shelf, Matthew joined his brother in the fun by climbing into another little locker, but eventually I corralled them and we piled back into the car. To occupy the boys today I had planned a visit to a nearby butterfly sanctuary.

En route, I drove through Hickory Run State Park. When I was a teenager, we had gone to that park once as a family, and it was still beautiful so many years later.

"I remember that little chapel behind the pond," I reminisced as we drove past. "It was here when I was a kid." The boys were interested in the miniature trucks they had brought along, so there was no reply from the backseat. The park road etched through the forest under a canopy of maple leaves.

"This is what I stand for," I murmured, to myself, as the car swerved under the trees along the windy route, "undisturbed land. This is what I want." I soberly considered that statement. Unspoiled land is one thing that I want my life to yield. Would it be better to take the gas-lease money, allow them to do what is destructive on my land, and then give the dollars to a charity to preserve land somewhere else?

At the sanctuary, I paid the entrance fee and we entered a magical room filled with flitting monarch butterflies, their delicate wings opening and closing above sooty black bodies. Even in my depressed state, I was enchanted by the scene. When Michael tried to grab the butterflies, a docent dipped a foam paintbrush in sugar water and handed it to him, and to our astonishment, a butterfly soon landed and began to drink. Matthew reached for one and we spent an easy half-hour feeding them as they fluttered gently around us.

Outside in the misty sunshine, I opened the picnic lunch while the boys climbed onto the benches of a wooden picnic table. As I focused on removing peanut butter and jelly sandwiches from the cooler, Michael discovered a wad of gum stuck to the underside of the table. Engrossed, he stretched it long and longer, until I noticed and snatched it from him. I wiped his hand, then began to slice the apples and open the can of cashews. Meanwhile, Michael had left the table and found a dirty, squashed juice box on the ground. As he leaned back to sip, I frantically yanked the straw away from his mouth. "No, no! Dirty! No!"

A raccoon or skunk had evidently hauled it from a nearby garbage can last night.

I repeated the wiping process and got them settled enough to eat their sandwiches, wondering if rabies could be transferred from juice boxes. Suddenly I felt very tired, and we ate in silence until a foul smell began to emanate from Michael's direction. I sighed and instructed Matthew to toss the food waste into a nearby garbage can, wearily wondering if our refuse would be on the ground by daybreak tomorrow. I spread a blanket across the top of the car trunk to take care of Michael's loaded diaper.

We headed home. Michael slept, and his head lolled from side to side as I negotiated the curves of the park road. Matthew also was dozing when, on the road ahead, I spied a little spotted turtle. I pulled the car off to the gravel on the side of the road. Matthew's head snapped up and he was immediately curious as I flicked on the car's blinkers and exited the car. Hurrying to investigate, I saw that its tiny shell had been crushed irrevocably onto the pavement by a tire.

The sight made me feel miserably unhappy, and being exhausted did nothing to improve my outlook. I heaved a sigh, hurried to the car and explained the situation to a seven-year-old Matthew. I finished with, "This is why I have been so sad; I want to prevent people from building roads that destroy creatures like turtles. If I sign the gas-lease, I won't be able to protect the turtles on our property. They could get squashed, too." Matthew looked suddenly confused. Tom had been telling the boys that they could have a go-cart if only Mommy would sign a gas-lease. Wildlife preservation hadn't been part of the discussion.

"I think that since the turtles cannot take care of their world, we are responsible, humans are, because we have the ability to do so. God commands us not only to have dominion over the animals, but to be stewards of them."

As I halted the car in our driveway, the silence of the engine surprised me, and I sat still for an instant. Protecting the land and all the little species at our little Wellsboro farm is what I need to do. If I cannot or do not protect my own land, how can I think of protecting other land?

Garbage in My Backyard

We are known forever by the tracks we leave.

—Native American saying

I carried Michael's floppy body to his crib so he could continue to nap, and Matthew ran into the house in front of me, searching for his crayons to color a butterfly picture. I returned to the car and leaned inside to grab the water bottles, the diaper bag, the bits of crackers that were lodged in the seats. *My car is always such a mess.* I pulled a wrinkled environmental newsletter from the floor. I had picked it up, today, at the butterfly center, but Michael had toddled off to grab the pushpins on a display board, so I hadn't read more than one line. I stood in the driveway, my hands filled with other trash, reading article at the top.

It was about wastefulness and how we (supposedly) use only one percent of the items we buy. *Ah*, I think, *I must emphasize this with Matthew—that we don't need so much STUFF!* How does one get a seven-year-old to agree with that thought? He loves presents and buying new things at the store. So do I, but how, when we are tired of them, can we possibly get rid of our things, if we can't put them in a garbage can to be hauled away?

When we were kids, we earned five cents for every glass soda bottle we returned to the ACME grocery store in Wellsboro, back in the days of button cash registers and S&H Green Stamps. Five cents translated to a big candy bar at Cuda's Deli on Main Street, so we collected bottles, dirty from gravel and weeds, strewn along our road frontage. For my brother, who took charge by sorting the bottles into old cardboard carriers and carrying them to the 'return' collection area in front of the store, there was fun in organizing a financially rewarding project. For me, it was about sorting out the confusion of where things went after we had finished with them.

Garbage was something I could never quite comprehend. Our paper trash we burned; it went away in a hot, smoky haze. Glass soda bottles we returned to the store for the bottle deposit refund. But what of the garbage? I saw my dad take the plastic bag filled with our garbage out to the curb every Tuesday. Where did it go?

"Into a landfill," my mother would answer, absently turning up the stove burner under the saucepan where a sealed plastic bag floated.

Ummm, corn, I thought, *my favorite*. Yet I was disturbed about the garbage.

Even now there is no curbside garbage pick-up at the farm, and residents have always hauled garbage to a dump. In auld lang syne, the farm dump lay in back of the fields, at the tree line, and there was just such a pile on the Penney farm. Luckily for us, it sat just west of our property boundary, so it became the problem of the 'other downstater,' as Mr. Penney called the new neighbor, when they bought the land. Once, long ago, we had climbed over the rock piles to explore the mess, but the new owners have since hauled the old washing machine, the rusty fry pans, and even the glass canning jars away.

When we lived in New Jersey, Tom and I had rented a house on a dairy farm and the stream below the barn was littered with shards of glass, cobalt blue or emerald green, old rubber gaskets, and rusty barbed wire fencing. On my walks, I would painstakingly collect handfuls of this garbage from the creek and its banks, to carry home for disposal, but there was always more, and it occurred to me that I was only transferring it from one dump to another, in some futile redistribution of waste.

In Wellsboro, the backyard of our little tenants' house also seemed to harbor a heap of garbage. Dad hand-dug a trench in the backyard to drain water that flowed from an intermittent spring located above the house. My mother, following him, picked up the bits of trash exposed in the earth. In fact, every shovelful was strewn with broken bits of glass, the fragments of porcelain dishes and rusty nails. According to Mr. Penney, there had been a 'rah-ute' cellar to store root vegetables such as carrots and potatoes behind the house, and this was the source of the broken jars that appeared in the soil.

Occasionally, Mom would uncover a whole bottle, and once, a miniature bottle with a tiny rubber stopper. I would collect the best, soak the dirt and grime off of their glass, and poke at the soil lodged inside, using little sticks. The perfect ones lined the windowsills of the little house: cold cream containers, pill bottles, a strange glass cup with a long narrow glass handle that my mother thought to be an old eyewash.

Now the contents of the root cellar would have included none of our discovered items, and I cannot imagine a root cellar behind the house, anyway, because the land doesn't slope in a way that might house one. I suspect that the backyard had been a little dump. Sadly, eviction, one shovelful at a time, is a slow process. Mom and Dad finished their drainpipe project, smoothed any bumps on the surface, and let the grass grow over the residual garbage.

Another question of garbage, though, lingered. What to do with the new garbage we generated there? Mr. Penney recommended that we dispose of our non-burnable waste at the ravine in the north woods of the Rawsons.

I stood by Dad's side near the wrecked autos that lined the driveway of tiny Mr. Arnold Rawson, who smiled and kindly offered us the use of his dump. My young mind couldn't understand the need for one. *Why not*, I thought privately, *just leave it anywhere along this slope?* The scattered cars and buses and old tractors wouldn't complain, and who would notice a little more stuff? Dad, though, thanked him, and for a few months hauled our weekend garbage to their dump. We tagged along, one day, and stared at the sight of the rusting cans, the old tires, the old mayonnaise jars tossed to the creek below. I wanted to climb down amid the rubble and pick out an unbroken specimen of an interesting bottle, but Mom would not allow it—a disappointment to my collector's spirit.

Dad was conversing with the youngest Rawson boy, who had some sort of automotive shop back here along the dirt driveway, and the talk was slated to be long. Conversations up here in Wellsboro always were. Waiting, Mark and I kicked an old Quaker State oil carton back and forth to each other, and when it was crushed by our blows, Mark kicked it into the ravine, grinning with delight at this unexpected freedom and power. He went to find more to continue his fun. I asked Mom who would ever clean this huge mess up, and she shook her head a little sadly, "No one, likely."

"Well, where does it go?"

"It'll likely stay here, forever."

I have struggled with this issue: Where does our junk go?

When I moved to New Jersey for my first big job, I was pleasantly surprised to find plastic recycling containers along curbsides in the bigger communities. Glass, aluminum, and eventually plastics, magazines and even junk mail were collected. Pennsylvania had nothing like this to offer, and enthusiastically, I volunteered for Saturday morning recycling days at the township building, glad that other people were worried about garbage, too.

The Rawson junkyard was eventually cleared, and though Wellsboro instated garbage and recycling pick-up at curbside, those of us who were outside the town limits had to haul our garbage to the transfer station. For two dollars, by hurrying through town on a Saturday morning, I could drop a heavy duty bag with bits of Styrofoam insulation, old shoes, and light bulbs—along with last night's chicken bones—out of my olfactory vicinity. The smelly bag fell into an open tractor trailer container located under the chute.

There were recycling bins for aluminum, plastic, glass and tin cans, and I used them all, until one Saturday I arrived at the dump to find the gates mysteriously closed. While the locals knew that the transfer station had been closed due to some DEP violations, it was news to me.

The nearest landfill was twenty-some miles away. *What was I going to do with my garbage?* The obvious answer was, "Take it back to New Jersey," and so we did. When Sunday afternoon arrived, we packed a bag of recyclables and an even smellier bag of garbage into the trunk of the car. We gagged when we finally reached home and unloaded the bag of non-reusable diapers to manage. In hot weather, hauling it ourselves was a smelly option.

As the summer progressed, I became more careful of what I tossed into the garbage bag, asking always, "Is this something we can burn in the fireplace?" Burning plastics produce dioxins, so plastics never went into the burn pile, but were piled in the utility room. Sometimes months went by until we had space to haul them home for recycling. In the meantime mice chewed on their edges and left droppings in the aluminum and glass jars.

What, though, to do with the little things: the Styrofoam meat plates and candy wrappers, the eggshells, the bacon fat? I concocted a makeshift compost pile and unloaded all of the vegetable and fruit peelings and egg shells there. It was a grand idea, except that the skunks got into the compost, since it wasn't much of a pile. Even though I piled grass clippings on top to hide the smell, there was inevitably evidence of midnight marauders in the pile. Eventually, I resorted to offending a few groundhogs by stuffing wilted lettuce and old watermelon rinds down their excavated holes.

Aware of these challenges, I made more careful choices when I bought food from the store. "What am I going to do with that smelly plastic pad that lines the meat carton?" Maybe we wouldn't eat meat this weekend. Living with my own garbage, with a sense that there is no place to put it, has made me aware of its inability to disappear by magic.

Diapers were a nuisance, but I managed to clothe our second son in modern cloth diaper pants, only using the toss-aways for nighttime. Still, the nagging reminder followed me that 'one-toss-away-per-day' would pile up, never to decompose. As I stared across the seared grasses of my hay field, I grimly acknowledged that, should I be forced to pile them in my own field, I wouldn't use them. Since I can dump them and forget about them, I do.

Eventually, the permit to haul garbage was reinstated to the transfer station. We can now dump again without any outside fetters, but my ways have been altered, due to the awareness inflicted by forces outside of me. It has become habit to minimize my trash, and some habits, thankfully, are hard to break.

I had forgotten, though, about the garbage shards in our backyard. One summer day, I plunged a shovel into the hard pan soil along the southern wall of the little tenants' house. What an excellent site for a kitchen garden: protection from the north wind, full sun, and close to the door for easy access.

What more could I want? After a few minutes, I knew: how about soil that did not contain rusty nails or broken jars?

On my next visit, I purchased a load of manure and a load of topsoil to make a raised bed. Tom and I drove my then-much-newer little car to the stone pile in the lower field and filled the trunk with heavy, flat stones. When the car body sunk to barely clearing the wheels, I gunned the engine to get the loaded car up the hillside. Tom ran alongside to guide me around the woodchuck holes. It took several trips, but Tom used the rocks to make the front wall of a flower and herb garden for me. We couldn't get rid of the junk, but we could have plants.

I closed the doors of my car and returned to Matthew and his butterfly coloring. In my arms I carried the refuse. It is easier to identify a problem than to fix it. It is easier to ignore a problem than to prevent it.

Back to Writing?

One cannot serve two masters, for either
he will hate the one and love the other, or
he will be devoted to the one and despise
the other. One cannot serve both God and
Mammon.

—Matthew 6:24

That night I served hot dogs for dinner. It was the best I
could do, I who used to think, before I had children of my
own, so ill of those lazy moms who served them rather than
making some homemade vegetarian wonder dish. All I can
say is, at least mine are organic hotdogs with no nitrites, those
being associated with stomach cancer. I can afford organic
food now, but what if Tom loses his job? By saying 'No' to
drilling, will I someday have to give up organic food?

After putting the boys to bed, I cleaned out that awful
hall cupboard; things avalanche out every time I open it. It is
the kind of job that I do when I'm alone and slightly stressed,
and it took over an hour. I extended my organizing spree to
the kitchen drawers as well. Somehow, my heart wasn't into
practicing piano.

Tom had called earlier, from Pittsburgh, and of course
the dreaded topic resurfaced. From his tone, I'd be willing to
bet that he discussed it with his parents and they sat around
and agreed that he was sensible and I was a whacky
environmentalist. He reminded me that the gas companies

would restore the land to its original state when they were through—a valid argument. Still, I resent that they discussed the ills of my position while I was not there to defend myself.

Now, purging drawers and closets, I plunged into my own mental gyrations. Will I be angry if the land next door is drilled, and I am forced to hear the noise, choke on dust and view the ugliness, and then, when it is finally returned to a semblance of its original state, I realize I have lost thousands of dollars because I did not sign? I will have had all the inconveniences, but none of the money.

As I packed a few bags of things to donate to charity, I reasoned that if the gas company would restore my hayfield to its original state after drilling—as they claimed to do—it would be no less natural than it was. *It really isn't a great ecosystem to begin with, anyway.* Maybe taking the money and allowing drilling was the smart choice.

It bothers me that the Commonwealth of Pennsylvania has sold gas rights from our state forests and game lands. Did we vote for this? Who allowed this? Does anyone spend their days petitioning the State House? I certainly don't. I slammed a cabinet door shut.

Well, could I change policy? How on earth would I do it? If it means starting vociferous protests in the streets, count me out. Way out. I hate crowds, especially angry ones. But could I work for an organization that promotes environmental awareness? I stared at the kitchen counter for a few minutes, and then tried to scrape a dried blob of cookie batter off of the cabinet with my thumbnail.

I want my belief system to be aligned with the goals and impact of any job I undertake. I also do not want the world's problems to be enhanced or passed along because I ignored them. I want to do something big, something positive for the environment, but I also have meals to prepare, books to read to children, and all the other home responsibilities. How do you juggle more than one full-time job? *Is* it possible for me to do two jobs very well at the same time?

If I am brutally honest, I thought, wiping my dirty fingernail on a wet dishtowel, I have to admit that the time with my boys is more precious to me than working 'for a cause.' I will not sacrifice my family right now. I have seen marriages falter because women are too busy, too drained from attempting to do too much. I do not want to fall into that category. We have worked very hard and lived rather simply for our whole marriage, and now the result is that I can stay at home to watch my children.

Couldn't I write a few hours a week? That was my plan, before all this gas drilling nonsense. Didn't I want to write about my childhood Wellsboro memories? So what if I don't work for an environmental cause? I tossed the bags into the chilly breezeway and flipped off the light.

But how can I forsake the wild strawberries and the bob-o-links singing on the grasses? And what of that enormous hawk that perched on the branches along the field, searching and swooping for its dinner? I shut off the kitchen light switch and went to brush my teeth. I was exhausted and it was nearly midnight … but I stared into the bathroom mirror, and twisted my lips, thinking, *I need to speak for the trees before it is too late, even if I have no time to do so.*

Take the Money, Bunny

Do not be lured by the lust for money,
and be content with what you have, for
hasn't it been written, 'I will not forget,
nor forsake you'?

—Hebrews 13: 5

On Sunday I read to the boys from their little Bible, the story of Daniel in the lions' den. When Daniel continued to worship the Lord in defiance of the law, it was surely suicidal, but he did it because he knew it was the right thing to do. Miraculously, the lions didn't eat him and he was spared. Would I be similarly reprieved for doing something that I knew was right? I doubted it. These gas-lease lions would not spare me.

As the boys went to play, I read a few New Testament lines, sitting on the rocking chair. "Do not be lured by the lust for money … Hasn't it been written, 'I will not forget, nor forsake you'?"

"I will not forget nor forsake you." Those were God's words. I kept repeating them aloud. And it *is* true; I am being lured by the possibilities of luxury and ease, the very thing I have accused my husband of doing. I must face the fact that it *is* greed, on my part. The lust for comfort *is* murdering the passion of my soul.

My mind wanders to a phone conversation I had this week. My sister, Natalie, thinks I would be in a better position to combat future environmental degradation by having a big wallet. She's right. So is the Bible's warning about lusting after money. Everything is getting hazy. The gas-lease dilemma is worming into my thoughts all the time.

"Land Ho! Land Ho!" Matthew started yelling from the bedroom, in a funny deep voice and inflection. I stood, stretched, and stepped into the bedroom. They have made a Noah's Ark out of Michael's crib, tying a basket on the side as a lifeboat for their stuffed animals. I smiled at them and did my part by fixing two small blankets as a roof; then I began to fold the laundry in the basket.

I keep trying to thank God that I am who I am and for giving me this test of fortitude. I pray that I might escape with my principles intact; then I could glide through life on light wings. How contented I would be if I could stand firm and say, "Absolutely not. Not on my land." But is it such a bad idea to give in? Ralph Watson—I need to speak to him. He has experience in natural gas pipeline work.

Karen and Ralph Watson returned my call. Karen is an old college chum and Ralph, her husband, is a full-time farmer who supplements his income by laying natural gas pipelines part-time. He is a big man, quiet and gentle, who only throws cows around by their tails when necessary. Strong-willed and confident, Karen had planned on being a suburban Ohio housewife, married to a man with a respectable white-collar occupation and living in upscale tract housing. Ralph turned her plans upside down—this rural Pennsylvania dairyman who plants corn at midnight rather than converting his fields into housing developments. How odd it is that Karen married the farmer and I, imagining rural life to be idyllic, was the one who married the respectable accountant who defines outdoor adventure as a round of golf on the manicured lawns of the country club.

Last night, after my closet-cleaning spree, I lay in bed, alone and exhausted yet mentally alert, sorting out yet another of my double standards. I have often harbored a tinge of resentment toward those city slickers who come to the rural suburbs to create a hobby farm—such as the 'lavender farmer' in New Jersey, with his spectacular stone barn. One Saturday I visited his farm and glimpsed within its walled field an antique farm wagon filled with fragrant plants and large glass jars of lavender flowers.

Rumor has it that the 'lavender farmer' is an ex-New Yorker who'd had enough of city life. From the brand-new machinery in the fields and rarely open roadside stand, it appeared that neither farm expenses nor tax bills relied heavily on occasional lavender sales to suburbanites. He who can play at farming with a bank roll set against the inevitable losses will face no big financial harm if a crop fails.

My mind contrasted that flexibility to the indomitable demands of farms that are run by lifelong farmers, with their barns deteriorating, their machinery rusting in the weeds, and muddy, pocked holes in their unpaved driveways. These are all signs of overworked people struggling to make a living.

In the darkness my face flushed with chagrin when I realized that I, too, am a hobby farmer. The owner of fifty acres of fallow land where I can pick wild strawberries if I choose, I, too, come to rural Wellsboro with hazy dreams of farming. I hire professionals to fix the sagging porch rather than do it myself and contentedly watch the grass grow during my vacations. I wonder if others harbor that same tinge of resentment toward me that I do for the 'lavender famer,' not as a person—I have met him and he is a very nice man—but as an entity: the rich newcomer. I guess they do. I sighed and rolled over in my lonely bed.

Ralph, though, was pleased to speak with me on Sunday afternoon. I doubt that he really thinks of me as a hobby farmer, and he isn't the resentful type anyway. I suspect he sees my farm as inherited land—which it is not—or a hunting cabin—which it also is not. At any rate, Ralph's advice was practical, and upon contemplation, I realize that it was given from the perspective of someone who his whole life has worked very hard for very little pay.

When Tom and I rented a house on a dairy farm, we observed firsthand how the dream of farming is preposterously easier than the reality. Dairymen work endless hours with little help and no days off. They are inundated with machinery that is in constant need of repair. Yet many still find time to serve as deacons and youth leaders and tithe as a matter of principle—these people who cannot afford time or money.

I told Ralph that I thought gas-drilling might exacerbate the environmental problems of our country, and that I felt that it was wrong to sign a lease. He laughed. "Your biggest problem is going to be how to spend that money." I said that I am the steward of this land I own, but that even if I continue to be a responsible steward, no good may come of it; the gas might be taken, anyway, via a neighboring well.

Ralph talked of religious faith and land stewardship. He thinks they are two different things, that land stewardship is secondary.

"Jesus is the way, not what we do." I know this. I did not voice a disagreement, but I think there is more to it than blind faith; we must act in accordance to our faith. I am sure Ralph thinks so, too, but does not see drilling for natural gas as violating the second part of God's command.

"Bunny," my nickname, "take the money," Ralph said emphatically. "If you don't, your neighbor will. If they drill within three hundred fifty feet of your land, your gas will be gone, and you will get nothing. Bunny, take it," he repeated. "Your biggest problem is going to be how to spend that money."

Ralph's parents own more than three hundred acres, but

they, like most farmers, are 'cash poor.' Ralph said that they were offered gas-leases a few years back and now have two wells out in the cornfields. The wells are a blessing to his parents, who had no retirement plan, short of selling the land. I told him that I had come to accept that there were people who would see this as a godsend, who would use the money well, and I didn't blame them, but that my situation was somewhat different. We didn't need the money, and I was too aware of the adverse effects of fossil fuel burning.

Ralph mentioned the old issue of cell phones and their towers, "I don't have a cell phone, so I can rail against them."

I realized that I am again confusing my friends, and think how hard it is to argue against something I use myself. We were raised in this lifestyle: gas grills, car trips in the station wagon, garbage bags, plastic toys. My little fiefdom doesn't run on solar power.

◈◈◈◈

Tom and I did have a wood-burning fireplace built in the little house so we could burn our own fuel. Years ago we found a local stone mason to fix the north wall of our bank barn, which had been bowing in. Larry prefers dry-wall masonry, which is what our barn has on three sides of the basement, which 'banks' against the hillside, but agreed to do our fireplace, as well.

One afternoon Larry arrived on his bicycle to deliver an estimate. As I reviewed his tiny paper scrap, with maybe four words and three numbers on it, I asked if we could save money by using the fieldstone on the property. I liked the idea of using what we have, and there were old rock piles in and alongside the lower field.

Mr. Penney had told Mom and Dad that a hay barn in the middle of the field had burned down many, many years ago; the rocks had been part of its foundation. As kids we climbed on those rocks, searching both warily and hopefully for sunning rattlesnakes. Mr. Penney told us how, while plowing, he would jump down from a tractor with a small hammer to crack small stones uncovered in the process. He'd haul the bigger ones to the side of the field. Tom and I used some for my raised kitchen garden, but there were still large piles at the base of the fields.

Larry shrugged at my suggestion. "You won't save anything. It would take a lot more time to pick the stones. Got to watch out for snakes, too … I don't like snakes." He shivered a bit, considering the thought. "I never liked snakes." After a moment he added, "It'll cost you more to pick the stone than to buy it, but my motto is, 'If you have the money, I have the time.' "

At the time, we had the money, so Larry had the time. Using our fieldstone, he faced a beautiful fireplace constructed around a fireplace insert. He made the mantel out of a brown, hand-hewn beam that had been lying unused in our barn basement. The insert, according to the manual, uses a catalytic converter to minimize pollution output, and the fan maximizes heat output into the house … in theory, of course.

Our fireplace project was completed eight years ago, when we were in the 'one-thing-at-a-time' phase of renovations. We lacked the finances and certainly the vision to make enormous changes, and having the time to contemplate allowed us to make decisions well-suited to us. After the fireplace was finished, we discovered that nearly everything else needed renovation: the wiring, the windows, and I wanted that awful tarpaper siding off of the walls. When the contractor took over and the repair work expanded like a hot air balloon, we often were required to make snap decisions. It is understandable, from a builder's perspective, but it did not allow us time to investigate the most "green" options or to carefully consider our own needs and wants.

I still dream of sun-heated water systems, but any such "green" improvements will not be part of the little house's future, not without a huge financial boost from me. Lately Tom has been insisting, "I'm not dumping any more money into the place, since you won't generate some easy cash from that very property." So much for going solar.

❦❦❦❦❦

I didn't get into all this with Ralph. Ralph likes to strategize and had some ideas of his own to share.

"Get the gas company to give you gas to the house, for life, and remember, the wells can go dry at any time. When the gas starts to flow, people expect it to pump forever, but it can stop at any time. I know you and Tom aren't the types to run up debt, but some people get themselves into a lot of trouble that way."

He continued his flow of ideas, suggested asking for a 'stump replacement fee,' for trees that the drilling company would have cut to put in the well. He acknowledged that it was something he hadn't thought of in time for his parents' lease. His comments indicated to me that Ralph is operating on a shoestring budget, and that the gas-lease companies write one-sided leases. The landowner must do his own research to find out what is negotiable, or pay an attorney to do it for him.

I voiced my concerns that the land would be destroyed, even after they removed the drilling rig. Ralph said that he and the other workers were very careful to restore the land to its original state, that the DEP was looking over every shoulder.

"We are especially careful when we know someone is picky about their land. They always come out and scrutinize what we are doing. Still, sometimes, but not often, there is contamination, and we have to drill them a new drinking water well." Ralph indicated that the well types were different in his part of the state. Where he and Karen lived, the oil and gas wells were "simpler, not as deep. [They don't use the fracturing process in northwestern Pennsylvania.] Some of the wells are dry," Ralph explained, "But these near you seem to be yielding gas."

When I quoted the dollar amount for our lease, he whistled softly. "They must have some Screamers … that's what we call wells that are producing big." I grinned in spite of myself. It *is* a great name, 'Screamer.'

Ralph closed by saying a prayer for me, which was oddly comforting and not embarrassing, as I had expected. Later, on the phone, I mentioned his sincerity and gentleness to Karen. She wryly remarked that I wouldn't consider him so gentle if I saw him tossing enormous cattle around by their tails.

Man Power

Later that night, with the kids safely snuggled into bed, I plopped in front of the computer and researched natural gas drilling on the PA Department of Conservation and Natural Resources (DCNR) website. Although I was apprehensive about prying into someone else's private material, the guidelines for gas operators are public information. I spent an hour or two reviewing the rules and diagrams on erosion control, which guys like Ralph utilized.

There were pages of engineering-type diagrams concerned with the layout of the drill site, the use of hay bales on steep slopes, and the location of holding ponds for extracted water. The water for fracturing the rock is transported to the site on big tank trucks, utilized, and then extracted again. It is stored in holding ponds until the trucks reappear weeks later to suction the water back into their storage tanks for removal.

The text assured me that there was a system in place for rendering as little damage as possible to the environment. The pages seemed to be quite complete, and I felt a surge of comfort. It was very scientific. There were responsible people who developed operating procedures for these processes. What could be wrong? With fifteen percent royalties on top of one hundred and thirty thousand dollars every five years, I would be a fool not to take it ... the fool on the hill.

I murmured, "With the money I could afford to fight back, legally, for any damage that they may do, or at least be a little better equipped to pay attorney fees." I closed the website and sat for a few moments, staring at my reflection in the darkened window, black against the night. I twiddled a pen nervously in my fingers, thinking about these standard operating procedures. They were complete, the assurance was there, but I felt uneasy and not sure why. I stretched my arms above my head, tilted the chair back onto two legs, and thought.

ᔕᔕᔕᔕᔕ

Before Matthew was born, my post-doctoral research was performed under the advisement of the Soil Fertility Specialist at Rutgers, The State University of New Jersey. We had performed extensive experiments on plant nutrients and crop yields at the Agricultural Extension Farms around the state, for crops ranging from field corn to blueberries. I loved being outside, and I learned to appreciate the challenges of working in the elements. I also developed a strong respect for those who do it.

Everything depended on the weather. If rain was predicted for Monday, we would drive to a far locale to harvest on a Sunday afternoon. Work depended on the weather, and so, consequently, did other aspects of my life. Making an appointment with the hairdresser could be challenging.

"Could you come to the salon on Thursday evening at 6:15?" A sweet voice responded to my call.

"Hmm," I mused aloud. "Well, that depends … It depends on when it rains. If it rains at least half-an inch on Wednesday, then I can make that appointment, because we won't harvest Thursday. But if the rain comes on Tuesday instead, or it only drizzles on Wednesday, then I can't make it on Thursday, because we might be harvesting late into the evening."

The dead silence from the other end of the line clued me in: I was speaking an incomprehensible language to this woman. She probably did not rub elbows with many women who did not wear nail polish, let alone those who gibbered about rain and harvesting. I could plainly hear the confusion in her silence, and as I lamely circumvented the awkwardness, I realized I had drifted into a world that was foreign not only to her life, but also to my own previous lives. In the industrial nine-to-five predictability of my pharmaceutical jobs, I hadn't even been aware of the weather once I was inside the building. Work certainly didn't revolve around the climate.

The uncertainty over scheduling appointments was a minor glitch. I loved the outdoor physical work and growing all those plants. The farm staff was always out there with us, tilling the soil, calibrating the seed planters, repairing anything that was hindering our efforts, dragging garden hoses to the field when the temperature was 100 degrees Fahrenheit.

My jobs have always been in predominantly male workplaces—as a chemist, student, and researcher—and, over the years, one thing I have discovered is that most men, though hard workers, will dodge some rules. They do it with satisfaction, too, particularly when they feel a requirement is unnecessary or unreasonable, and most seem to disregard warning labels. I once watched in horror as my own tax accountant husband dismantled the safety features of our lawn tractor, so it must be genetically influenced, and not career specific. Time and again they do it, until they experience, even second-hand, the ramifications.

I dropped the chair onto all four legs and snapped my fingers. That is what bothers me about the diagrams of operating procedures: The men! Which rules do they value? Which are to be taken seriously? What potentially disastrous short-cuts are they willing to take? What will these workers do when the state regulator is not on site—when the DEP's back is turned? I sat in the quiet room, now less assured by the hay bale diagrams, doubting that Ralph's perspective was more valid than my own.

Working

Joy's soul lies in the doing.

—William Shakespeare

Memories fade. My recollections of Dad arrive fleetingly and depart soon after; he has been gone for so long. When I do pause to remember him, I vow to put more time aside, to recall his words, to maintain that connection that still exists, yet I do not, and I worry that he will grow ever more distant.

The memory of his hands, though, is still vivid; I can conjure the feel of his work-roughened fingers and the smoothness of his fingernails. Both of his thumbnails were 'flat'—wider than they were longer. One of my thumbnails is like that, too, and both of my sister's. I read once that this genetic variation is deemed 'the mark of genius,' which steels me whenever anyone stares, then blurts, "Hey, look at that! Your thumb is so weird. How did *that* happen?"

I don't like attention that invariably sets the population of a room gawking, but I do not mind my thumbnail. It is perhaps an odd connection with my dad, but it reminds me of his hands holding carpentry tools.

৵৵৵৵

One early summer we helped Dad shingle the 'long side' of the saltbox roof in Wellsboro. Ostensibly, only Mark was going to help, but before long, both Natalie and I were up on top, pounding nails energetically. The roof had been covered with a thick, spongy tar-paper—no shingles at all—a neglect Dad attributed to the fact that its appearance was not visible from the road. Mr. Penney had never seen fit to outlay the cash for the job, but Dad had plans.

Mom stayed home during those few days of roof work; aunts Betty and Dottie were due to drive her up later. Dad filled his nail belt with flat-topped roofing nails, lifted a pack of floppy shingles onto his shoulder, and up the ladder he went. So up we followed with little hammers in our little hands, to be in on the action.

Dad taught us how to overlap each shingle over the preceding one and how to stagger the notches evenly. We grabbed old coffee cans filled with nails and soon were pounding to our hearts' content. Later, as Dad paused on the ladder, surveying our progress, he exclaimed, "I can't believe how much we have accomplished, men! I can't keep you supplied with enough shingles!" I glowed with pride and sunburn.

We rested near the roof peak, then after lunch worked steadily all afternoon as Dad cut the pieces for around the chimney and Mark helped to haul up the shingles. There was a rhythm to the work, hammers beating upon the roof. The next morning we worked even harder, bent on finishing as much as possible before Mom arrived in the afternoon; we wanted to surprise her. Seasoned laborers now, we hurried about with confidence.

The car pulled in, and Mark and I waved. "Hi Mom! Look at us!"

She craned her neck. "Hi there!" she sang out. "Good to see you! I missed you."

"We missed you, too!"

She had wandered around to the back and there was a pause as Dad reached her. "Oh … *All* the kids on the roof? Do you think that it is a *good* idea?"

Mark returned to his work, while Natalie and I chimed down, "We're fine, Mom!"

"Well, don't get too near the edge!"

"We aren't."

"Well, *be careful* up there."

Mom, with her avid fear of heights, continued to spend the rest of the afternoon on the ground, asking us to come down or admonishing us to be careful. We dismissed her worries with slightly aggravated tones.

Her frequent interventions were distracting and took a lot of the pleasure from our work, but my lasting pride in having helped shingle the roof almost made me forget the last part of the story. Last year it resurfaced, too vividly.

Tom had gone up with a tar bucket to where the new addition linked to the old roof, and Matthew had delighted in following him out the window, scurrying around that very roof on all fours. Soon he was on the peak, grinning down at me, as I stood with Michael playing in the grass at my feet.

"Look at me, Mom!"

I looked. My blood chilled. "Be *CAREFUL!*" I yelled up to him. "Don't get too near the edge." I had not suffered hours of labor pains to lose him this way.

"Oh, Mom, I'm *fine!*" He scuttled around the new peak of the roof.

"Matthew, stay away from the edge and watch that electrical wire! It is very dangerous."

"Mom, I am not near it."

"I know, dear, but please, *be careful!*"

"I am fine." His voice thinly veiled his annoyance.

Questionable Valor

Valor is a gift. Those having it never know for sure whether they have it till the test comes.
And those having it in one test never know for sure if they will have it when the next test comes.

—Carl Sandburg

I called Mike Gallo early. It was the second time in three weeks I had called him in distress, and when he answered, I dove quickly into the topic of that cursed gas-lease.

"Mike, I am oscillating violently, one side to the other, and that shift is very surprising to me. How can I be so sure at 3 p.m. that I couldn't live with myself, should I take the money, and then, at 9 p.m., be so sure that *not* taking the money is pointless?" I hurriedly prompted him, "You're the psychologist type. Is this one of those phases of mourning: denial, anger, whatever?"

"Well, it is helping you with your decision process, and finding a middle ground, no pun intended." He sighed and added grimly, "Trouble has found you."

"Yeah, but I don't have to give it a chair."

"It already has a chair sliding under the table. It's coming for dinner, Stephanie."

"Mike, I would allow it, I fear, because it is easier to take the money. I fear that taking this money would give me a cushion, and I would do none of the things I always planned to do, such as write a book or try to grow my own food, simply because I would no longer have to do them … It's easy to make yourself do hard work, even boring work, when you need the money, but it'll be easy to be lazy with this chunk of cash in the bank!"

"It is only a cushion if you decide to use it as a cushion," Mike said quietly. I suddenly realized that he had hit upon the crux of the matter. When there is money to shield against ramifications, it is easy to drop projects and look to the next great idea.

"It cannot just be because it is easier to take the money, or else you will not be able to live with that decision." He paused. "What is the silver lining in this? This is a growing experience for you." I told him that I am trying to be glad to have this decision to make for myself.

"What a great thing that a friend with morals is being asked to make the decision!"

"You're watching your friend's morals decay." I acknowledged, ruefully.

"NO, I am watching my friend's morals in play!" he contradicted. I was comforted by his belief in my nobility but not convinced that he was right. The greatest people in the world do not concede.

"Mike, I want to be the hero in my own story!"

"Steph, there are no heroes in this scenario. They are comin' under your land! You are not preventing pipes from coming under your land and taking the gas! You cannot stop them. That black-and-white thinking is gone. It's out the window! Your book is about the realities of vanishing resources and the effects of people's choices. That black-and-white book is out the window!" he repeated emphatically.

Amazed at his succinctness and accuracy, I said nothing. 'Vanishing resources and the effects of people's choices' sounded quite impressive to a woman who has spoken monosyllables to children for eight years. After a lapse, Mike's voice softened, breaking the silence, "Listen, I had two responses initially. First, I thought like Tom, that the financial pressure would be off. Really, that is a big thing, especially for me, since I am not married. Then secondly, I would think, as you did, that I hate this crap I am in, and I wish it would go away."

"That is a problem. Aside from the environmental impact; I want all conflict to disappear."

"You cannot stop it." Mike moved to a more realistic aspect of the topic. "Steph, use the money and sabotage them. I've been thinking: you could take the gas-lease money and twist it into a resource for an environmental group that works to stop mining and drilling. Look, it is foolish to lose the natural resources, but it is also foolish to lose the dollars that are rightfully yours."

"I don't feel as if they are my resources to sell."

"There are rules and structures as to who can take what, and we abide by them. Someone is coming to take them and since you cannot stop it, you might as well be compensated for it."

'Compensated,' another big word. My brain *has* deteriorated. How could I ever write a book?

"Look, you can consider these dollars pay for raising your voice. They've taken someone with morals and values and given her a platform. Our society values status and dollars. You could write a book and show people what it is to be tormented when it is on your own front lawn. This dilemma is strengthening and deepening your environmental value systems as you wrestle. Listen, I have got to go; I am at the parking garage. I'll call you next week."

Gray Area

The ends are achieved by indirect means ... a remark made by a teacher in the middle of a discussion, a book picked up in someone's room ..."

—Harold Taylor

Michael was playing on mosses under the red pine trees by the fence, wearing only his pajama top. Earlier he had refused to change into day clothes and then had later the notion to partially undress himself. I glanced around in the sunshine, then back to see him pushing pine needles into little piles. I recalled how I had decided to make writing about Wellsboro a priority, and to forget the academic positions for now.

And then, just as I had started this nightmare plopped itself down and stared at me. Maybe this is an opportunity to do what I want, to write about it, I thought. I don't even know if I can write a book, even one about this gas-lease challenge. Why, what will the ending will be? I snorted to myself as potential titles flashed across my mind: Fool on the Hill, One Woman's Excuse for Raping the Land, or Fool on the Hill, One Woman's Ideals Result in Nothing. Did I even have the whole picture?

I recalled, with a twinge, PJL and my PhD qualifying exam. PJL are the initials of my PhD research advisor, Professor Paul J. Lioy. His initials are how the students referred to him behind his back. I think this type of non-provoking slight is generally due to the uneven status of student and advisor. Thesis advisors control the academic futures of students, and the inequality rankles, so the students take the liberty of covertly nicknaming their professors.

With PJL, though, I think I understand some of our consternation: he appeared, on the surface, to be an athletic, casual guy, the kind you can joke and chat with; however, being a physicist with a complex, inaccessible mind, it was hard to discourse with him on any subject.

"Physicists are chemists," a chemist colleague once deadpanned, "without the charisma." We could not understand him, and so PJL's comments were often received by his students with much subversive eye-rolling.

Now, the function of a PhD qualifying exam is to determine, before allowing students to invest further study time, if their academic strengths outweigh their weaknesses. The exam itself is particularly mentally grueling, as the administering faculty is not nearly as interested in ascertaining student strengths as they are in discovering student weaknesses. Thus, during the three-hour oral exam, subjects in which a student radiates knowledge are immediately terminated. It is rather demoralizing to be warming up to a happy little lecture on the laws of osmosis, only to have a professor interrupt to pose a completely unrelated question on the intricacies of modeling stream flow.

I was distinctly relieved that during my qualifying exam, my faculty committee didn't uncover much lacking in the academic regions of my mind. However, when PJL chose to speak that day, he was, for once, completely comprehensible.

"You think," PJL tented his fingers in front of him and enunciated each syllable precisely, "too much like a chemist." He paused and glared at me through thick glasses. "Chemists are linear thinkers, digging vertical holes in the knowledge, but never glancing at the horizontal spectrum that gives it perspective." He spread his fingers widely, leaned forward and slowly concluded, "You must stop thinking like a chemist, Ms. Hamel, and begin to think like an environmental scientist. You must consider the ramifications of environmental decisions to all of the associated parties."

PJL might not be popular with his students, but he was excellent at targeting weaknesses. My penance was mild in a department where qualifying exams generally resulted in more coursework for the student candidates. Instead, I was asked to review written material from a variety of perspectives—regulatory, literary, and political—because it was concluded that I was naïve about the economic and social considerations of the field of environmental science. They wanted me to consider the range of the field. I am beginning to wonder, though, all these years later, whether that extra reading actually corrected the deficiency.

ഊഊൟൟ

Last week, I had called my brother-in-law, Scott, to ask about hybrid cars. I will soon need a new car, and, with my newly-awakened environmental conscience, I want to do the eco-friendly thing. Scott spends a lot of time overseas, where he works to remove kinks from the automotive computer software that his company develops. He is skeptical about the environmental friendliness of hybrid cars.

During our conversation, Scott mentioned the cost to the owner, but then, sensing that wasn't allaying my enthusiasm, he asserted, "It is the batteries … They are nickel cadmium. The damage caused by mining those minerals outweighs any environmental benefits yielded from saving on fuel."

I didn't ask him for his sources; likely he reads industry trade journals. *Well*, I wondered, *which is worse: mining or combustion emissions?* I suppose it depends on which one, if either, exists in 'your own backyard.' Is one of them harming you, your children, or your parents?

Scott concluded, "Those batteries don't always last more than 100,000 miles, and they cost a couple of thousand to replace." My brother, also an engineer, had said as much.

So the decision to buy a hybrid car, like allowing gas drilling, is not simple. It is easiest when things are black and white. What complicates matters are the gray areas: that there are undeniable benefits from combusting fossil fuels gathered from under my land, that batteries for hybrid cars are made from materials gained via questionable mining practices. The best thing would be to stop using cars and natural gas, wouldn't it? But really, is that going to happen soon, without a struggle?

My mind traveled for a moment into the vague realm of effectiveness. At times, to be effective, one must make choices that have long-term benefits but are detrimental in the short-term, and vice versa. We keep animals in zoos, which is hard on them, but zoos preserve species and foster an appreciation of animals in the wild. Think of plastic medical equipment, which fills up landfills yet extends countless lives and alleviates suffering.

I recall a professor in graduate school who mentioned in passing that his brother was visiting from Greece. "My brother noticed that Americans like to have one good guy and one bad guy, all good or all bad ..." He paused and added wryly, "I observed the same trait when I moved here, fifteen years ago, but it stopped seeming unusual to me, the longer I lived here."

Over the years I have thought of his observation. If I heard this comment again, I would reply that America is a young country, with untapped reserves of natural resources within its borders. Because of these, we are wealthy and can afford to be idealistic and demanding, wanting 'Yes' or 'No' for a quick and complete answer. Our nation has—and rests comfortably on the foundation of—ideals.

There is no gray area about my status, though: I have been converted from a rather uninformed consumer existing within our society's structure to—potentially—the known facilitator of actions of which I disapprove. I have seen the natural gas drilling sites and yet I continue to grill chicken. This is clearly a NIMBY case: Not In My Backyard.

Michael called for my attention. I looked around dazedly as my thoughts left the old graduate school days and the more immediate gas-leasing issues. I took Michael's hand, wiped a pine needle clinging to his adorably chubby bottom, and wandered with him through the sunshine to the house.

Acute or Chronic Issue?

We mutually pledge to each other our Lives, our Fortunes, and our Sacred Honor.

—Thomas Jefferson, The Declaration of Independence

At lunchtime, Tom called from work, and we discussed the issue, again, seemingly for the millionth time. His voice was hollow with sadness.

"I wish we were aligned on this. Your refusal to sign affects me, as well. You know you entered into a contract, fifteen years ago, financial and emotional."

"But that 'contract' was for better or worse, richer or poorer," I sputtered. "There is nothing stating that I had to earn every possible penny to make you happy." I leaped a decade into our marriage history, "We want to maximize our free time and minimize the stress. We agreed that I would take care of the children. If I had a full-time job, I would come home to the same demands that I have here all day. Being here allows me to tackle most of them during the day. Even your free time would be greatly diminished, because you would have to grocery shop, do laundry and prepare meals. I do all that, now."

"But you are living a contradiction." Tom's argument took a different tack. "You say that you don't want to promote fossil fuel burning, but I don't believe that it is a principle for you, because if it was, you would be living it."

Previous forays down this path had spawned further rumination of the subject. This time my response was quick: I blamed our society. "But we were raised to be consumers! We didn't learn at age six or seven to conserve fossil fuels. I am slowly working myself into that; I can't easily give up our means of heating, cooking, and getting around. That may sound hypocritical, but that is the reality. I simply do not own a wood cook stove and the use of them is nearly a lost art. Besides, burning wood is polluting, too. There is no easy answer, unless you want to go back to nature and eat only raw foods that I can forage."

Your family thinks I am strange enough as it is, I thought, but did not add. I could just imagine the sideways glances and covert gossip, should I decide to wear homemade deerskin clothing and contribute dried pemmican to Christmas dinner.

"I am reverting from trained consumerism to minimal-impact living, albeit slowly. I compost all our fruit and vegetable scraps. I shop in thrift stores for blankets and clothing. I have neither the interest nor patience to be terribly fashion conscious, so I'm not so much a victim of that kind of marketing anymore." I rattled off my list, now better formed in my head than in our last 'you are a hypocrite' conversation.

"Some things are easier to do, now that I am not commuting an hour to work. I can hang the laundry on the clothesline to dry. I can find the time to make homemade bread and soak beans."

Not that we eat many beans, I concluded in my head.

Tom drifted to another line of thinking, much like the qualifying exam committee. "I understand the economics of the energy industry. They are out there, developing the next thing—wind, solar, whatever. It is in the best interests of these companies to do so. It will help them survive in the future. They are building, using the fuels we have today, to change things for the better, tomorrow."

I paused for breath before jumping again into the silence. "Well, we don't know what the potential damages to our land will be if we do allow drilling. We might have radon spewed into the air from these wells, or God knows what! You're looking at the short-term—the more predictable, and therefore more manageable, financial considerations."

Our discussions truly have spotlighted that Tom and I are observing different angles of the same scene. I tossed out an analogy: "The Emergency Room doctors are trained in acute care, while environmental researchers are concerned with chronic health conditions and their prevention. The two groups do not have interchangeable perspectives and cannot deal with the same issues. You wouldn't hire any old Emergency Room doctor to single-handedly devise a plan to prevent an epidemic. That is the difference: one looks at the acute damage and the other long-term damage; neither is wrong, but neither has the entire picture."

I love analogies, but Tom is more literal. I paused, half-expecting him to start spluttering that I was making no sense whatsoever: we were discussing natural gas-leases, not emergency room visits. When he didn't, I continued.

"I have pondered this enigma in other situations. Look, Tom … Logically, in a life-and-death situation, there is no need to consider the long term. Long term might not be a reality. However, in 'not immediately life threatening' situations such as this, you can rely on the experts who understand how to prevent exposure to the things that cause the illness in the first place. It could be cigarette smoke, or radon, or molds, whatever. If you don't eliminate the source of the problem, and if you don't maintain the most ideal health, a problem will likely recur. That is where my experience and education are leading me to say 'No' to the promotion of the drilling of gas wells. We do not know what the long-term negative impacts are to our land or what is coming out of the wellheads, and so it is best to not expose ourselves and our land to these potential negatives."

"But, Bunny, the Third World is being helped more than being hurt by fossil fuels. Look at China, or India. These businesses create jobs and better living for the people. Listen, your goal to end fossil fuel usage will be met eventually because these energy companies will want to corner the market. It is human nature. There is no striving toward success if society is not rewarding success. Society will be helped, if we do this. I truly believe it."

I diverted this truth by challenging him to think about our own situation. "Well, what if you had to make the choice for our next-door neighbor? He has the potential for making the money and you don't. He can do anything to that land, have three wells dug if he likes, and you have to watch it all from your front porch. What do you want him to do?"

"Well, he took the risk. He should benefit from it."

"Tom, you didn't answer my question. What would you want him to do?"

"He'll do what is in his best interests."

"I didn't ask what he would do. I asked 'What would you want him to do?' "

"So my answer is a non-answer. I would want them to stop driving those trucks up and down the road." He paused, then added, "I think he would spend dollars and it will be good for the economy. I would benefit indirectly, too. Maybe he'd put another pond on his property where I could fish. I will benefit, some way … Listen, I don't think that burning fuel is bad. If we are paying less for fuel; then people will pay more for accounting services."

"Given the lay of our property and its shape, it would be less invasive to have a well drilled on our land than to have it put on the next-door neighbor's. We can't see beyond our barn because of the rise of the hill, and the well site could be placed way over that hill. We wouldn't even be able to see the damage to our land from the house, but if they drill on his, we could."

He returned to our personal situation. "Listen, Bun, you'd be upset if I said, 'I have to golf every day of my life; I don't want to work anymore,' or 'I know it is selfish, but my soul is convinced that it is right: I must golf every day, so I must quit my job.' I can't do that, though, because I have to think of you and the boys. By not signing the lease, you are, in effect, forcing me into exchanging my life for money, for a longer period of time."

I sat, miserably silent, understanding. I had worked at jobs I didn't like. It is awful to face an undesirable situation, knowing there is an easy means to escape it.

"Listen, Bunny, you have to make the final decision, but if I do something wacky, I don't want to hear about it."

I perked up, startled.

"*Wacky*, like what?" I spat out the words. "*What?* What would you do that is wacky?"

"Listen, if you did suddenly engage in behavior that you could stop, that was not positive to the relationship, I would have a rational reason to divorce you."

I tried to grasp his meaning.

"Are you saying that you would divorce me for one hundred and thirty thousand dollars?"

"No, I didn't say that. I am just thinking that it will cost me a few extra years, and I am likely going to resent that." He spoke slowly and emphatically: "What I mean is that I intend to golf *every weekend*—both Saturday and Sunday—for *the rest of my life!* And I don't want you giving me grief about it."

Luxuries Money Can Buy

Next morning, I spent an odd moment scratching a list of the luxuries that I might be sacrificing, the travel dreams, first:

1. A Hawaiian vacation.

2. Spending a year in Scotland, and then seeing the gardens of Wales and England, the beauty of Ireland.

Michael's vocal demands diverted my attention, so I threw down my pen and took him on a short walk, down to the pond across the road. We sat on the swing awhile, I musing and half-heartedly listening to his chatter.

I felt I was overlooking something that Tom has given to us, something I couldn't identify, yet shouldn't ignore. Tom has never really balked when I want to buy an item that he didn't value himself, and we rarely have even a small row over money. And this isn't a row, even now. This is a very distinct disconnection between what we believe are morally acceptable ways to earn money. We see each other's viewpoint—also that neither of us can be dissuaded. One of us will have to concede. That is what is so tiring: we see the opposing perspective, know we are not going to agree, and realize that neither plans to yield.

It is more than that, though, I thought, as we jumped off the swing and walked toward the sunshine. As I wandered past the hemlock trees along the driveway, I thought about all I have gained by living in this rather wealthy locale, of what we might have to give up if Tom's job ends and we have to transport ourselves from here. Here in Northeastern Pennsylvania there is a sense of community. It is tightly knit in a way I have not experienced since childhood. Practically everyone knows everyone else and—while there is plenty of historical gossip to learn about your neighbors—they care for each other, and for strangers. Here, they galvanize into action at the first sign of need. I find comfort within such an enclave of politeness and kindness.

Yet to stay in this community, or any community, I need money. I wouldn't be welcome without it. I need to pay my bills, or have my husband do it. There is the reality: we need money, and while I walk through the sunshine with Michael, Tom is busy, working for us. In fact, today he interviewed for a job with a medium-sized accounting firm. It seems inevitable that his present job will disappear before long.

When he arrived home for dinner, handsome in a business suit, he was rather subdued.

"The pay would be two-thirds of what I am making now, and I would be senior tax manager, not a partner."

I bit my lip and looked away. We both know what that means: long, late working hours, seven days a week, nonstop from January to April 15. *Dealing with all that again, that harder life, is not something I can face at the moment*, I thought, as I scurried about, getting dinner on the table.

Later, we shared an ice cream bar, the last one, and discussed things. Tom talked about the stress of public accounting and concluded quietly, "I cannot help but think that I am going to resent what you are doing. I wish I wouldn't, but I will. We could have this money, which is rightfully ours."

I could only put my head in my folded arms on the table and whisper, "I know. I'm sorry."

He chomped the last bites of the ice cream bar, and a few minutes later I lifted my head from the table and went to the bathroom to soak in the tub. Beautiful green-blue water spills noisily out of the tap, likely tinted by copper salts leaching from the pipe. The acid in the soils from the hemlock trees acidifies the water and—if my understanding of inorganic chemistry still holds true—after resting in old copper pipes, the copper is converted to copper sulfate. Whatever its chemical structure, it stains the washcloth and my towels blue.

I wondered if the copper was zapping the zinc from my body. I had once read that low levels of zinc can lead to depression, and I certainly am feeling low. I scrutinized my fingernails but saw no white spots, which the article suggested was indicative of low zinc levels. I don't even want to think about the lead solder in the pipes. I concluded that the gas-lease was bothering me.

Earlier in the day, idly swinging by the pond with Michael, another idea had popped into my head, which now resurfaced. Perhaps I could make a little money—some of what we will lose by not signing the gas-lease—in order to make it up to Tom. I could research scientific articles and translate them for more popular media ... or I could write about this gas-lease dilemma. Yes, I could do that.

I enthusiastically climbed out of the warm water and pulled a towel around me. Then I sighed. *Who was I kidding?* I didn't have time to research current science and start a new career of journalism nor did I think I'd have a reason to write a book, if I sold out.

Maybe I will sell out.

I pulled on pajamas, kissed the sleeping boys in their bedroom and walked into the living room to plop next to Tom on the couch.

"I can't sell out. If I can't protect our land, our fifty acres, what is the point of saving other land, through charities, with all the money we get? This is the land I have to protect. I think it's wrong to take the gas money."

"It isn't wrong."

We discussed it a bit; then Tom tried to kiss me, but I was sad and serious. He got up and went to the kitchen, saying, over his shoulder, "We'll figure it out."

Slightly comforted, I turned on the old laptop computer and started typing from my current diary: my so-called gas-lease book manuscript.

Arrowhead

And the thoughts of youth are long, long thoughts.

—Henry Wadsworth Longfellow, "My Lost Youth"

I held my breath and stared at the smooth stone lying flat in my small palm. The sun shone warmly on this blue-streaked black rock, which was so different than the yellow-gray crumbly rocks that I usually uncovered. Surely it couldn't be, and yet it was … I knew it was. I exhaled slowly, turning it over and feeling its sharp edges against my skin. It was, beyond a doubt. How could I, a nine-year-old girl, have found an Indian arrowhead?

I had read of arrowheads and spear points, and had kept my child's eyes peeled for them, wherever I walked. In vain I grabbed twigs and pried under soil to remove triangular rocks, only to find clumsy outlines that confirmed they were not arrowheads. By strange chance, today, I had spotted this stone and leaned over to uncover treasure only a foot from the newly-dug pond.

❧❧❧❧❧

It was Torpy's pond then, and we were there at its inception, when the Army Corps of Engineers expanded the small pond that was fed by our spring. We missed the actual bulldozing of the old chicken houses and movement of the soil—we only visited every few weekends—but when we awoke one Saturday morning, Natalie and I discovered an enormous bowl of mud in place of the old pond. Its bottom contained water, and Dad assured us it would soon fill to the top.

We raced to the edge of the water. Red brown mud squished between our toes and, sticking our hands into the soft clay, we rolled little mud balls. The pond was sheltered from the west wind, and the warm sun beat down on us as we played, burning our legs and arms and reflecting from the muddy water onto our faces. The mud spattered us and Mom laughed, suggesting that we simply put on our bathing suits, rather than soiling any more clothing. We looked at each other, did just that and spent another glorious hour back in the mud.

"Just like pigs," my brother snorted.

The pond eventually filled, and by the next spring, tiny black tadpoles swam in the shallows. We trampled upon sweet smelling mint as we tried to catch those 'pollywogs,' as Mr. Penney called them. Only until the Torpys built a floating dock and smiled on our using their rowboat did we stop lamenting the loss of the mud.

How had this arrowhead remained on the very top, the tip-top of all the soil banked to trap our spring water into this pond? How could it have survived the machinery's heavy tread, and why had I stooped to examine it? Was it the smoothness of the stone, or its unexpected color?

And how was it that I had found this valuable treasure, not on a museum shelf under glass, but here, where the sun was hot on my neck while chilly wind whipped and tangled my red-brown hair? I held no less than my own discovered proof that ancient peoples had hunted long ago right here! Running my fingers along the nicked edges of the shaped stone, I could imagine the forest revived. I looked around me, half expecting to see the fields subdued with dappled light and an Indian hunter, quietly tensed next to the spring, waiting for game.

Why am I fascinated by the tools and fragments of another lifetime? It is evidence, undeniable evidence that legend was truth, truth that long dead civilizations once roamed this very spot. I pushed the strands of hair from my face and, taking shallow breaths, ran barefoot to the house with my treasure, to share its magic.

Economic Plunge, 2008

September 18, 2008

It is chilly in the mornings—long pants weather. Afternoons are warm in the sun, but soon I must stow away the shorts. Tom has a meeting out of town, so I drove Matthew to school and then played with Michael on the school playground.

When we moved here, Tom drove Matthew to a Montessori school, which is close to his work. But first I had called the transportation department to see about public school buses. The manager informed me that Matthew would have to take at least two, perhaps three buses. Not wishing my kindergartener to negotiate even one transfer, I agreed to Tom's plan of driving him ourselves, hoping we could find another family with whom to carpool. That was not to be, and anyhow, as I discovered after Michael's birth, two car seats are the capacity of the back of my car.

The swing at the playground creaked in the stillness of today's valley mist and it was lonely, just the two of us outside a school filled with children. We soon departed for the grocery store to buy milk and a few other items. As I deposited Michael carelessly in the front of the cart, I stared at the newspaper rack—at the black headlines that had grabbed my attention. I snatched one, then another. The news of the plummeting stock market blared from each of them, and I fingered the thin pages uneasily.

In a daze I wandered the store aisles. I know that I do not look our monetary situation squarely in the eye these days. I let Tom do that, I, who used to silently mock women for not knowing their own financial conditions. I know now why this happens. With the care of children and household duties, there simply is too much to be done, so some responsibilities need to be delegated. If a man is willing to take care of finances, let him. If he will help cook and clean, too … why, that would be even better.

What does this mean for us? What are the implications, financially? Am I a fool for not trying to gain financial security when the world is plunging into uncertainty? My dad once told me that I must learn to look out for Number One. I bought two papers.

Back at home, while Michael napped, I read the papers with mounting unease. My steady resolve to resist the gas-lease had evaporated; maybe we would need this money. After Michael woke, we dropped over to see my friend, Madeline*. I haven't spoken to her since school started, but with this national economic upheaval, I needed the comfort of another soul. She thinks we should sign and take the money, and at least use the money to get off the grid or buy a hybrid car. My head agrees with her thoughts, but my heart doesn't.

As I leaned into the car to re-buckle Michael's car seat, I said, over my shoulder, "I must decide if it's better to live by my principles and have no positive impact, or to act in a manner, using the drilling money, which might result in my being more effective in promoting my principles." I stood up and stretched. "Right now, I am not ready to compromise my principles."

Dinner that night, though outside on the porch, was a little gloomy. Tom told me about his day and of the mounting inevitability of his job loss. We finished the meal rather quietly. I said, "Well, one of us is going to be bitter about this gas drilling money. Do I want it to be me?"

Tom, however, dragged me back to the practical aspects with a dose of financial reality: "We will need money for retirement. Your pension from Rutgers is worth less than

$8,000, and our future needs at retirement, according to my prediction, will not be met by my savings in the 401K plan. Social Security will be a bad joke by the time we get in line for it. If I am fired, we will have to buy our own health insurance. My car bill today was over $1,300, and tomorrow yours will be $1,000 for the new muffler and exhaust."

Stinky old car, I thought.

Peeking at Peak Oil

It seems to me—as so often in a woman's life—I am asked to think out an abstract problem when I am very tired out with a multitude of infinitesimal concrete and immediate problems.

—Anne Morrow Lindbergh, *War Without and Within*

September 19, 2008

Oddly enough, I greeted the new day with no burden of sadness on my chest. For the first time in days, I was aware of how nice it is to wake, in the night, and snuggle closely to Tom's warm body before drifting back into dreams. I felt released of a burden. The guilt is gone.

The day passed in the usual duties: diapers, laundry, meals and dishes, running errands. After the boys were in bed for the evening, I reviewed an old newspaper editorial that I had clipped. The author did not attack or support gas drilling, but looked past the present boon of natural gas. Her article, apparently one in a series, presented the idea of Peak Oil and its ramifications to our lifestyles, or rather, the ramifications for our descendents. Peak Oil means that there is a point when accessible oil will have plateaued. It will be followed by a future where there is less and less oil. Once we have depleted our resources, we may lose our ability to generate so much cheap energy from the internal combustion engine.

"We might no longer be able to travel so easily, nor haul our food supplies."

The whole thing was sobering, a cold dose of reality. *What a hardship that would be*, I thought. Still, it was excellently written: factual, not emotional. I was finishing when the phone rang. It was Tom's college roommate, Mick Ley.

Mick and his wife have been visiting for summer weekends in Wellsboro for well over a decade. He was the laid-back one in Tom's college circle, well attuned to social issues. He rarely calls and I wondered if there was a problem. Since he gave no indication of a crisis, and doesn't initiate chatter anyway, I took advantage of his reticence and explained the gas-lease conflict. His reply arrived before Tom put down the golf club he was swinging in the living room to wander over and take the call.

"Well, I think you can use the money to restore the Penney house on the farm. The groundhogs living inside there need an upgrade. Or the money can be invested to take the place of five years' salary. Tom could retire early." I had thought Mick would be more on my side because of the environmental angle. I pushed him on the subjects of fossil fuels, global warming and pollution. He admitted that he doesn't have a problem using fossil fuels; he just doesn't like the way we get them. I'm not sure if he means the war in Iraq, coal mining, or both.

I passed the phone to Tom, so they could talk and I could think about Peak Oil. I doubt that my friends and neighbors think so pessimistically, but I have this haunting feeling that we are on top of the global heap merely because our country still has an abundance of natural resources to deplete. Once that supply diminishes, where will we be? I believe we can best avoid tripping down that pathway by altering our strategies now.

So, what do I mean, exactly? What would I say if someone in the media called and asked, Dr. Hamel? Probably, "Uh, could you hold on a minute? Boys! Shhhhh! Mommy is on the phone!" Then what would I say? I am not even sure what 'cap and trade' is. Who and where is Dr. Hamel, anymore? Is she simply buried under piles of dirty laundry or has her mind completely deteriorated?

Do I mean that we should depend on America's resources rather than import anything? If I do, that means that I should be promoting the extraction of my own gas. Well, that's not what I want, for sure. What do I want? I want us to use less of the world's natural resources than we currently do now, regardless of who owns them or where they are.

My own state government has leased thousands of acres of forest land to the energy companies. If my interpretation of webpage publications is correct, the various conservation groups are not taking a stance against the drilling. Am I alone? Can one person, saying 'No,' make a significant difference?

I ponder this, as I have for the past troubled few weeks. Can I stop the gas drilling on a large scale? No, I can't. That is true and frustrating. It is also true that my acting alone will not alter anyone else's viewpoint, because they will be unaware of my position. Do I want fanfare to lead an environmental revolution? No. What exactly do I mean by 'significant difference'? I don't know, and am too busy and tired to unravel these thoughts properly.

I went to bed, deciding to circumvent the mental wringing of fossil fuel issues by reading a few pages of *Environmental Health Perspectives* instead. Of course, its cover article had to be about carbon footprints. I was scanning it when Tom joined me. Apparently Mick was upset because his wife had flown to Tennessee for a week to help her sister-in-law with a new baby, leaving him home to juggle the kids and his job.

"He was feeling irritable and wanted to complain to another male gorilla."

Tom leaned in to read over my shoulder for a minute; then, as he rolled over to sleep, he teased, "*I* want to have a big carbon footprint … *big foot.*"

I smiled and flipped off the light switch.

Luxury Loving

Old and yet ever new, and simple and
beautiful always.
Love immortal and young in the endless
succession of lovers.

—Henry Wadsworth Longfellow, "The
Courtship of Myles Standish"

The next night we attended a most elegant wedding at an
historic hotel, a quintessential Pocono manor. The lodge,
a magnificent place for an elegant wedding, was built on a
grand scale with cobble stonework.

Mom arrived in the afternoon to babysit so that Tom
and I could enjoy the evening together. The boys immediately
sought her attention, so she and I had only fragments of
moments to speak. During one of them, Mom advised me to
sign the gas lease: "One cannot stop it; might as well take the
money," and "The money could be put to good use." My
thoughts thus were tainted with the gas-lease conflict even as
I settled in my seat amongst the other wedding guests.

The bride could not have ordered a nicer evening for her
outdoor service, and she was beautiful in her finery. We sat in
the back and watched the procession of very young
bridesmaids and groomsmen. The groom looked so baby-
faced that I almost burst into laughter at the absurdity of such
a little boy getting married. I had heard that he was a medical
doctor and she was twenty-seven. Just when and how did I get

to be so old that twenty-seven seems so very young? I wondered about it, dazedly. I have been so absorbed in the world of child-rearing that I lost track of my own timeline.

We knew no one at the wedding, save Jim and Helen—the parents of the bride—so, after the happy vows, Tom and I were free to roam and mingle at will. At dusk we strolled along the garden beyond the bocce courts. Seeing a gazebo at the summit of a mountainside in the distance, the Scottish Highlands came to mind. *Well, that was years ago, too,* I thought, *when we were in Europe.* I haven't traveled via plane since then, not with children to complicate vacations.

I felt a pang of discouragement as we wandered back to join the happy revelry of the crowd with their drinks and chatter. A seven-man band was playing as the waiters hurried and guests searched for dinner seats. We passed the display of family wedding pictures. The fresh one was of the newlyweds, the bride slim and elegant, her long thin arms graced with flowers. Next to it stood older, faded wedding photos of their parents. Jim looked unrecognizable and funny in his outdated glasses and full head of hair; Helen was beautifully slim and as lovely as her daughter, the bride of today. Would we, I wondered, staring at my reflection in the picture's glass, be hosting our sons' weddings someday? Would they be an echo of their dad? And what kind of wedding would we be overseeing? I rubbed my finger against my lips, a nervous habit.

What money indeed is needed to fund such an extravagant wedding? If I did sign a gas-lease, we would be able to afford this—a smashingly fine dinner for three hundred guests and cocktails all night. We wouldn't choose this kind of party, but it was rather disturbing to think that I could be jeopardizing the possibility of such a luxury.

I am just watching the money slip through my fingers.

I turned to Tom morosely. "It is beautiful here. I would love to make it possible for us to afford such a wedding for our boys, but I don't think I can."

Tom squeezed my arm, to comfort me.

These thoughts were put aside during our attempts to maintain conversation with total strangers at dinner. Later, on the dance floor, we saw a woman, very tattooed, dancing nearby in the arms of a beefy man. Tom leaned over and whispered, "I am going to get an oil derrick tattooed on my arm, with the words, 'could'a been rich' under it."

I looked into my husband's eyes and giggled with relief that we could joke about a topic over which we so disagreed.

Who's Supporting This?

I find that the great thing in this world is
not so much where we stand,
As in what direction we are moving.
To reach the port of heaven, we must
sail—
Sometimes   with   the   winds,   and
sometimes against it—
But we must sail, and not drift, nor lie at
anchor.

—Oliver Wendell Holmes

One morning I smiled as I said to Michael, "I'm going to get clothes on you," but swinging his arms and standing naked, he chanted, "No tank yohoo, Mah-Mah! Me hide!" and scooted out of the bedroom, giggling. I delighted in chasing him, scooping him up in my arms and kissing him as he giggled, but *what* did I do with the rest of the morning? The days always seem to fly past, blurring together, really.

Perhaps this kind of fuzzy living is inevitable: chasing one's child, finding balls and tossing them. It is improvisation, unscheduled, and fun. It leads to exploration. The difficulty is that its value cannot be quantitatively measured.

At least at night I get some mental work done. Last evening I was startled to discover a newspaper article posted on the Internet about a bill in the Pennsylvania House of

Representatives, H.R. #2453, which would alter the current Oil and Gas Conservation Law. This law, if I understood correctly, would require the installation of meters to monitor gas released from the well, and—more pertinent to us—require owners to be compensated if drilling occurred under lands not covered by a lease agreement.

I was excited by my find and called out to Tom, who was practicing his golf swing in the living room. As I waited for him, I read the final piece of the bill addressing the conflict between those landowners without mineral rights and those who owned the rights.

"Well," I murmured, "Thank heaven we never had to deal with someone else owning the mineral rights under the land we own! That would be the worst: watching the landscape and trees decimated on your very own property without being able to stop it or profit from it.

"Now let us hope that something will be done to save the gas. Maybe if we stall the leasing company, this bill will pass and the decision will be easier." Tom read over my shoulder, then commented briefly while focusing his attention on a scratch on his seven-iron. "This will take too long. It will be two years until they pass something."

"But, by then, it will be too late," I cried. "Everyone will have signed up, already."

Tom gripped his fingers around the club and widened his feet into a golf stance.

"That is the way the government works. They fix the problem after it is too late, and want credit for trying. Why do you think the tax system is so screwed up?" He cocked his chin to one side and lifted his club before continuing. "It's why you never hear of any unemployed tax accountants. What do you think: is my hip swinging too far out when I lower the club?" I raised one eyebrow then flounced back to the computer screen. Even if what he says is true, I was encouraged.

℀℀℀℀

The next day Michael and I built a train of wooden pieces. I checked my e-mail, then called Harrisburg about the gas drilling bill—plunging into strange, new waters. I was cautious. Would a representative from Wellsboro identify me as a troublemaker? I was afraid that I would be discovered to be a naysayer, the only naysayer in the region, *and* a flatlander, at that. Are all these lawmakers in cahoots with the energy companies? Would I be labeled a troublemaker and, in some Russian KGB way, be punished? Might my car be nudged into a ravine some dark night? These dramatic and chilling scenarios inspired me to be vague when a secretary took my information: that I was interested in supporting legislation to revise the current Oil and Gas law. She promised to have someone call me.

I herded Michael outside into the bright daylight. I appreciated the trees—magnificent greens, oranges and reds—and we both enjoyed the warmth of the sun. He asked me to carry his tiny bucket of golf balls, and he hit them as we walked toward the fence. Back at the house, I hung up the laundry on the porch clothesline, then rested with Michael as he napped and curled his warm little body against my shoulder.

After he was sound asleep, I went to the computer and searched for the phone number of the only person I know who has any experience in the elected government: Jane, a woman whose daughter went to school with Matthew. I had chatted with her in the school parking lot one afternoon. Her ex-husband was a Pennsylvania State Representative. As an attorney, she might also be able to offer advice.

I dialed the number and she answered, so I managed a quick explanation for my call and a question. She answered: "Well, legislation has little to do with your morality. You must go with your ethics. If you don't want to drill, don't."

I smiled inwardly. Hers is the type of mind that I encountered frequently while working in the chemistry lab. Scientists are often perceived as cold-hearted and calculating, perhaps because of their direct, unfiltered speech. Yet their style of communicating reflects a way of thinking: linear and concise. By nature or training, we cut away extraneous material to get to the source. Jane is of the same ilk.

In one sentence, I told her about the Law of Capture and why my morality might do nothing to protect the gas from being extracted and burned. I then mentioned the bill in the Pennsylvania House of Representatives: "I tried to call the one representative who was sponsoring the bill. Someone from Lycoming County, I think. How do I know if this is the right thing to do? Are they in cahoots with these leasing companies? What if I get a bad rap somehow, if there is a negative comment about me? What could you recommend?"

"Find out which special interest groups are involved. Forget the reps. Concentrate on the special interest groups."

"Find out who is supporting the bill? Like the Sierra Club?"

"Yes."

The brief conversation reminded me that my brain has gone fuzzy. Michael's chubby little arms around my neck all day make me forget how to think concretely.

As I drove to town, I was discouraged and almost ready to sign a lease. A month ago I had scrolled through several conservation Web pages. I had expected them to condemn the drilling outright. I was surprised to discover that they were remaining neutral, even dancing around the issue! I decided they must be fearful of the industry lobby.

Impulsively, I called Tom on my emergency cell phone.

"Tom. I am afraid of what the gas industry will do to me if they find out I am against drilling."

There was a pause before he replied, "Uh, listen … I am really busy here. Can I call you back?"

"Listen, I just called the government. If the gas companies think that I am trying to promote reform, they may hire some goons to harm the children—you know, to silence me."

There was silence on the other end of the line.

"Did you hear me?"

"Silence you? *What* on earth are you saying? *Who* would want to silence you?"

"The gas industry of course! They might start following us. They might tap our computer through the Internet, or stage a break-in, to intimidate us."

There was a heavy sigh on the other end of the line. "Listen, Bun. You sound like these paranoid doctors. They hate each other and think their conversations are being bugged by the others."

"This is serious business, though. The gas companies don't want anyone standing in their path."

"You're nuts."

"I am not. It happens whether or not you believe it … What was the name of that movie … I can't think of It … it happens—intimidation. Don't be naïve, this stuff happens!"

"Why would the gas companies hate *you*? They *love* you. You are giving them our stinking half-million dollars' worth of gas for free! *Who* wouldn't love you? *I* am the one you should watch out for."

The secretary from the state representative left a message a few days later. She was calling to ascertain that I had, indeed, been contacted by a knowledgeable assistant, and that my questions had been answered to my satisfaction. I never bothered to refute her inaccuracies: no one had ever called me from her office. I gave up chasing that angle.

Practicalities and Impracticalities

> When formerly I was looking about to see
> what I could do for a living …
> I thought often and seriously of picking
> huckleberries…
>
> —Henry David Thoreau, *Walden*

October 2, 2008

I pulled the gas-lease paperwork out of the cabinet and scanned it. There is a promise of payment within ninety days of signing, but not a demand for the return of the lease within any time frame. I wish I could talk to Frank's pal in Susquehanna County; he might recall how long he was given to sign the lease. I'll have to find time to put in a call to him. I don't want to call to arrange a meeting with the gas people without having an idea of how long I can stall about a decision.

On the computer, later, I caught a video news clip on the Marcellus shale. I suddenly thought, as I always do when I see the publicity, that we could be making a fortune. My greed slithered over me like a snake. I wanted that money and I hated my greed.

"But," I reasoned to my willing soul, "My car won't likely make it through the winter. The fumes inside the car are awful, and every part seems to be wearing out." On my way to pick Matthew up from school I craned my neck as I drove past the hybrids at our local car dealership.

I would have been completely depressed if we hadn't been taking care of the neighbors' animals while they were away. A brown hen escaped from the wire fence and Matthew asked us to help herd her into the henhouse, a chase we all found amusing. Then, when he went back to check on them, Matthew spoke soothingly to the chickens. It was adorable beyond words, and I thought, *We should live on a farm.*

When the kids were in bed, I returned to the living room to propose to Tom a way to spend less money, now, to take the pressure off him: "We should purchase a farm."

Tom sliced his pitching wedge through the air. "We already have one."

"Should we move to Wellsboro?" I thought it was a reasonable suggestion. "We could save eighteen thousand dollars a year in rent." I wistfully recounted Matthew's interactions with the farm animals.

"We would be on top of each other; that house is way too small."

True, I thought ruefully. I said that if we fixed up the Penney house as a garage and an office for Tom and built a ramshackle cabin in that copse of woods near the old garden—for my projects and maybe for writing—we would have enough room. We only had to be creative. I had found plans for a simple one-room cabin, and Matthew could help build it. What a great experience it would be for him!

Tom snorted. "Don't drag me into any more of your projects. Every time you get started, I end up wasting valuable golf time helping."

He addressed his golf club: "She wants a little writing cabin, does she? We need ten thousand to tear down the Penney house and fifty grand to fix the barn, and now she wants a writing cabin?" He turned to me. "*I* know a way to get a hundred grand. Try *that* and I will think about it." He swung his club again. I wrinkled my nose with a tolerant frown.

A few moments later he added, "The winters are long."

"Maybe we should move to North Carolina," I piped. I have suggested that before, but haven't gone down this route for awhile.

"We could live there for six months, and go to Wellsboro for six. We don't have to live the way everyone else does, just because it's traditional. We could be old people, but with children. We could home-school Matthew ... and," I raised my eyebrows at him, adding archly, "*you* could golf year-round."

Tom ignored the suggestion and began to list the practicalities. "We need health insurance. We need to have some income. We need money for retirement. I have no contacts in North Carolina, or Wellsboro, for that matter, who could supply the necessary client base." I stared at the fire for a few minutes then got ready for bed. The house was very chilly on this cold, crisp night. The crescent moon and the evening star set behind the mountain, as a bird, in silhouette, skimmed along the top the mountain, heading due south. I dreamt of Wellsboro.

ཀ་ཀ་ཀ་ཀ

The next morning Tom left early to go golfing. In the afternoon he joined us at the park. On my way there, I left a pint of blueberries at Madeline's house. Madeline had e-mailed me a magazine article on gas drilling in the Catskill Mountains. I was pleasantly surprised to read that there is a strong contingency of people in the New York metropolitan area who are opposed to it, and have even proposed a moratorium on gas drilling. Of course, this will not help my situation in Pennsylvania.

I also recognized a distinct flatlander versus local

opposition in the article: the weekender wants the serenity; the local wants the same financial wealth as the weekender. Who can blame either? It's just like the 'lavender man' versus the 'local dairy farmer.'

Madeline's husband brought their children down to meet us in the park, and Tom hit tennis balls to all four boys, as I sprawled nearby, relaxing on the warm surface of the court. Rex* stood, uncertain if he should join Tom. I could tell he'd rather be reading the newspaper folded under his arm than chase tennis balls and decided to put him at ease: "Don't feel obligated to join in. Tom is in his element. He loves this." He glanced once more at the happy boys and settled onto the warm ground before proffering a section of the Sunday paper. I lifted my reclined head but declined his offer.

After a few minutes he poked a finger at an article on future fuel technologies. Rex can talk much more intelligently on the subject than I, and yet, here I was, the research scientist and he, the salesman. I am always dismayed at how much better versed Rex and Madeline are than I on the applications and 'big picture' of science. A favorite chemistry professor had once said in class, "We are learning more and more about less and less." I think of how truly that applies to science and other aspects of our world. I am often tongue-tied when trying to converse about science issues. In the past, my mind was always too narrowly focused to look at the whole picture, and the sour truth is that I don't mind not always being current, now that my world is so small.

Rex told me that his mother had been offered twenty thousand dollars for a gas lease on land about a hundred miles east of Wellsboro. "The whole family thought it wasn't worth it." Rex's relatives are artsy people who work in New York City, in costume design and television production, and come out weekends to relax. He asked, philosophically, "How much difference do you think it will make in your lives, really? That place is our place for repose, to relax and we don't want anything like that in our yard."

I wondered if having extra money really would change the way we lived. What would we do differently? If we had the money, it would help us buy cars that are better for the environment and maybe a windmill to supply our electricity for the farm. But what else would we buy?

That evening Matthew chased the chickens into the henhouse and insisted that he do the chores and collect the eggs by himself. It was fun to watch him take such interest and show mastery of his tasks. I am proud of him, but it took so much time. Dinner was, like last night, black bean soup, but tonight no squabbles arose from the boys eating their food, though Tom and I started to bicker as we cleared the table. He wanted to begin working on tax returns for the October 15 deadline, and I was simply too tired to do the dishes and give the boys baths and do their bedtime routine by myself. In my opinion, instead of going golfing, he should have gotten his work done this morning, so he could help with the boys at night.

Rights and Wrongs

Nearly all men can stand adversity, but if
you want to test a man's character, give
him power.

—Abraham Lincoln

October 6, 2008

I called Frank McLaughlin. I need to know the time frame
for playing out this gas-lease charade, and Frank's buddy
might have some clue. Michael was ripping my papers, so I
had to get to the crux of the matter.

Quickly, I updated Frank on the situation, concluding
with, "Well, I hate to have to choose between wrongs, but that
is what I must do."

He contradicted me. "You have a choice between 'rights.'
You have a 'right' to keep anyone from touching your land,
with a 'right' to determine what the future of that land will be.
You also have a 'right' to sell the rights to fund your
children's education and your retirement."

Frank, who is usually boisterous and jocular, suddenly
became reflective. "I didn't think you needed the money so
badly that you would sell the land rights. Are you that
desperate? Both you and Tom have the ability to find work,
and especially Tom. The world will always need tax
accountants, no matter what the economic forecast." I agreed,
but here was a person with a big state pension looming in the

future; I doubted he grasped the precariousness of the financial futures of those without his security.

He encouraged me to get a teaching certificate. "The schools are screaming for science teachers. You could totally out-compete anyone. With your education, you could teach Earth Science, Chemistry, Math. You'd be great."

No, I thought, *you would be the great teacher.* He would be. Frank has that easy manner and personality that students love, and he has a genuinely caring heart that they would trust.

I told him I would likely be mowed down in a classroom handgun incident because I don't intend to ever back down on a grade again. "Besides," I added emphatically, "I don't want to be inside a classroom all day, teaching electron dot structure. I couldn't face another day of teaching electron dot structures!"

"Teach Earth Science; you'll get outdoors," he replied airily. "And if you get your certification now, you'll be ready to teach when Michael is in kindergarten. You are just what schools are looking for."

I grimaced and returned to the subject at hand, namely his friend who owns two nurseries on the Route 1 corridor, near Princeton, New Jersey.

Frank took up my lead. "Jeff and I are on the Shade Tree Commission, and I see him about once a month. He is probably busy this time of year, but he is a very interesting person, a Rutgers grad. You probably would have a lot in common, the same viewpoints on things, and likely know some of the same people."

I brought him up to speed on some of the information I had gathered about the gas leases.

"Sounds like you know more about this than Jeff does," he said. "He was offered a couple hundred dollars an acre in the spring but was reluctant to see his haven desecrated. Now they are offering him much higher amounts and he isn't sure what to do."

I discussed the differences between rural Pennsylvania and New Jersey. "Frank, in New Jersey, everyone is aware of how valuable land is. There is a limited amount, and everyone is packed in like sardines. Here in northern Pennsylvania, we have open space and I think others don't see how encroachment is taking over, slowly but surely." Realizing the time constraint of the conversation, I didn't go into my world population diatribe. The world's population is growing exponentially, and resources are increasing in value. Land is going to be an incalculably important asset in the future. Frank, as a remediation specialist, already knows that.

"Well, in upstate New York they have wind farms and are looking into solar farms for the future. Stephanie, your farmland may be valuable not only now, for the gas underneath the land, but in the future—not only as farmland, but also as solar farm land. Residential land has not increased, but farmland values have increased twenty to thirty percent in the past few years. Prices will go even higher, with the land having the potential to be more valuable. If your land and water become contaminated in the gas-drilling process, you might have to pay to have it cleaned up."

With that prompt, I asked about the DEP, in Pennsylvania. "How do I uncover information about a gas company's violations, and how does the DEP react?" Frank said that the DEP had search engines to find out who was 'in violation.'

"Call the Williamsport office, or the Scranton one. They will have the information and will also know about the legislation. Learn about the company who is drilling. Maybe they have links or can e-mail stuff for you to examine."

Frank ended with the conversation with, "Listen, you value the land for other things. There is value in the history for you, and as a retreat. How can you put a number value on that?"

Sourly I replied that, with everyone around us turning

the land into an industrial park, it didn't have much value as a retreat.

Half-Baked

By the time I do,
Half the things that I want to
I'll have another list that's twice as long.

David M. Bailey, "Another Song"

October 9, 2008.

At last, here was a warm Wellsboro weekend—an Indian summer afternoon, the sky blue above and the trees all coppery reds and greens and golds! Tom had taken the boys golfing, so I plopped down on the old rocker on the porch to begin to read a book Louise had raved about and lent me about six months ago. When I called to report on the unwavering production of the strawberry plants she had given to me, she had seemed disappointed that I hadn't read the book yet. I have a two-year-old; I don't sit much.

Today, after reading a well-written passage describing what it was like to try to eat locally for a whole year, I became discouraged. Here was a woman who has done the things I dream of doing: she became a professional author, and she grew most of her own food on her own farm. *My projects here*, I thought, looking across the expanse of Wellsboro lawn, *are only part-time attempts. As a matter of fact*, I grimaced, *it is part-time everything for me: part-time here and part-time at home.*

My glance stopped at the wild patch near the hedge: our

makeshift vegetable garden. I frowned at it. I should have weeded more, before the weeds got out of hand. Tom had laughed at my weed-patch. I do not have enough time here on the weekends, and then we have to leave.

This morning Matthew and I discovered a row of fully grown carrots, almost hidden, while we were digging potatoes and garlic. I love homegrown carrots. In other years what I grew had been spindly little excuses for them. We were so surprised to unearth several pounds of long orange ones. Matthew was as delighted as I was.

"Mom, let's call it, 'The Garden of Surprises'!" he exclaimed. It is fun to be aged seven again, with him. At least I am teaching him something about growing plants and I am promoting his enthusiasm. I smiled at the thought and glanced comfortably at the book in my lap, only to have my thoughts turn immediately pessimistic, taking the shape of sarcasm. *Oh, and I can see it now ... Let's check the fly-leaf— she probably has already dealt with and written about the gas- lease issue and is on her way to saving the world through better alternative energy. With my luck, her book will be published next week.*

Thinking about other writers I admire and their books reminded me that I envied the so-called simple life of *Little House on the Prairie*. This afternoon, in this beautiful warm sunshine and autumn colors in the trees and grasses, I had proposed again to Tom that we live here, if his job disappears.

Tom bluntly reminded me that the kitchen walls in this little house are not insulated. "We *would* be living the shanty life of the *Little House* books."

I suppose the idea is unrealistic. Once the leaves are gone, November is a dismal month. The winters here are long and the skies are gray. I wished we were on the other side of winter.

Geese honked in the sky, gliding down to light on the pond. Such a noisy clamor. I thought of Ruth Harper, the blueberry lady, saying to me, last fall, with the wistful wisdom of the elderly, "The sound of geese in autumn is such a different sound than that of geese in spring."

Could we stay all summer, and migrate south, like the birds, for the winter?

The boys came back from golfing and then hurried off to fish, which was a bonus for me! I could catch up on my own writing. First, I dropped the book on the rocker and hustled inside to start dinner. *Shoot, what a foul-up.* I thought we had pasta in the cabinet. I always have pasta lying about, so I didn't buy any at the store yesterday. I searched feverishly in the refrigerator for a substitute and decided on our garden potatoes, carrots, and sliced pork chops.

I heard Tom and the boys chattering excitedly at the pond as I hung the wet dish cloth on the clothesline on the back porch. The fish must be biting. The sun had set, and the world was orange and yellow gold and deepening greens—all except that incongruently stark white pearl of a moon above the barn. The crickets were chirping rhythmically. What a moment of perfect peace and beauty it was.

I sat on an old chock of wood that we use for a door stop on the back porch. The rustling of the long, cream-colored leaves of corn, the rattle of the tawny aspen leaves, and the echoes of a car shifting on a distant road settled around me as I scribbled hurriedly in my journal to capture all of the sights and sounds before I was out of time.

Then tired Michael began to cry, and Tom soothed him, "Dada will hold you in a second, Michael," before recasting his own line. The boys were starving, and my dinner and writing were half-baked, but at least I had sliced our own homegrown carrots for dinner.

Moral Dilemma of All Dilemmas

Courage is the price life exacts for granting peace.

—Amelia Earhart

The house is a wreck, with bags of apples, half-washed dishes, and laundry in piles. It always looks like this when we come home from the farm. I easily ignore it all, once I get outside, and instead admire the view across the pasture, but inside the house, all the projects leap to grab my attention. When am I going to wrap and send the iris rhizomes to Louise, or find information about fixing my popcorn popper?

This month's *Environmental Health Perspectives* issue arrived, and I fished it from the mail pile rather than wash the dishes. I try to scan it every month, to keep my brain in gear. The cover page subject was 'Ice Calving on Ellesmere Island.' Global warming makes the science news, but I guess I understand why fixing pollution and global climate change aren't tops on 'to-do' lists. For one, it isn't noticeably affecting us—at least here in PA—and secondly, we don't believe that any individual's efforts can offset the problem. Also, we are too preoccupied with the challenges of our own daily lives, the acute cares, to set time aside for long-term 'earth planning.' Even for me, the day was too beautiful, so I dropped the journal and ventured into the woods. Michael climbed on rocks, held my hands and jumped off, counting "One … two … one, go!" which made me laugh. I taught him

"One … two… three, go!" and then I silently mourned that he had stopped counting in his old, baby style.

Back inside, I lay with him until he fell asleep for his nap and thought about what to make for dinner. We will probably have salmon; it's not awful, but I just don't want it. I am too tired to be virtuous and only eat fish to feel good about eating healthily.

Mike Gallo called, a welcome relief from meal planning, to ask about the leasing issue. He ruefully commented, "Everyone has something that they bounce their heads against," and spent a few minutes describing an analogous situation. He had been taking a foreign language class in college. One of the students informed him that she was a sales representative for an Italian company and asked if he wanted to work in California for them over the summer.

"Stephanie," he said plaintively, "at age twenty-two, I, Mike Gallo, who had always wanted to travel and see the world, decided to give up an all-expenses-paid trip to the bikini-clad coast of California. All I was to do was visit the beaches and bars, stroll up and down, and chat with the people I met, and of course, I was to promote their product."

That sounded great, I thought. I remembered wanting to venture out to distant lands after college, but I was responsible for student loans, and besides, my dad had terminal cancer. I had to choose: either see my dad, or see the world. Mike's parents were healthy; his father is still working as a professor.

"Well, why didn't you? You could have spent your free time touring the whole state!"

"Well, the Rutgers woman was my friend, and I didn't want to disappoint her."

"She thought you would do a good job. Did you have to be their best salesman?" Mike always was fastidious about the moral issues.

Mike paused, then dramatically blurted (and incidentally

reminding me of his father's toxicology lectures), "Because it was to promote cigarettes! The one thing that I cannot stand is cigarette smoking. My grandfather died of emphysema and my grandmother was addicted to them. I wanted to go to California, but I just couldn't justify pushing cigarettes on people …"

Mike dropped his past conflicts and added, "This gas-lease deal is your moral dilemma of all moral dilemmas. And it is tough. I told my mom about it and she said that their Cape [Cod] home was her sanctuary, and it would feel sullied if she was asked to damage it."

I asked him if I was thinking with my twelve-year-old brain, the one that wrote letters to the federal government—in sixth grade—urging it to promote alternative fuels.

"You have retained your values and you have grown with them. They are still yours."

That was a nice thing for him to say, but if I sign the blasted gas-lease it won't be true.

He talked about how aging and change is gradual, like hair loss, and I chimed, "It is like the ugliness of electrical wires across the landscape … We don't notice how ugly because we never knew what it was like prior to the telephone poles and wires."

He agreed, "The gradations are small, day-to-day … This is tough; we all have these things. One day you wake up thinking one way, the next, another. You could be cruel to yourself and give yourself a deadline."

He paused a moment, as if hitting on the clincher, "You have to live with this every day. Therein is the answer. There is no perfect scenario. If you decide to sign the lease—and and you can sleep at night, knowing this is not black-and-white—then you will have made the right choice."

I scrawled all of his comments on a folded piece of paper, the backside of a request for a charitable donation. I had to write in between the paragraphs on the front as well. "Make the decision that I can 'live with in my head, always,' " I scribbled as I murmured. Mike concluded, "Listen, adults seek security in the form of money. Your gas field is my cigarettes. Everyone bangs their head against something."

Special Interests

Honor wears different coats, to different
people.

—Barbara Tuchman

October 16, 2008

When everyone else was sleeping, I found information on
natural gas sites on the Penn State University
Extension website in *The Landowner's Guide*. Its photos
revealed the reality of the industrial site created by drilling,
which, in some odd way, comforted me.

*Ah, here is something about placing restrictions on
exploration on the surface*, I thought. I definitely need to share
this with Tom. I raced to our bedroom where he had fallen
asleep while reading.

I tapped his shoulder. "You have to read this, all this
legal stuff about leases." He grunted and pulled the covers
over his head. "Listen to this ..." I began again.

"I read tax crap all day. Let me sleep."

I climbed onto the bed with the printed document and
continued to read. There was something about it being illegal
to drill under property that is not leased. I leaned toward the
night stand and grabbed a pen. I underlined that statement.
In the same paragraph, I read that the Marcellus shale had to
be hydraulically fractured to release the trapped gas, and that
this gas commonly was released up to a thousand feet from

the borehole. I double underlined 'a thousand feet.' That meant that the gas drilling site was on our doorstep. They might not drill, but they might send down explosives to crack it. How many feet in a mile? 5,280? I was too tired to remember.

Next evening, as we were doing dishes and getting the boys into the bathtub, some Executive Committee member for the local Sierra Club called. Unfortunately, with the clamor in the background, I never got his name, and I couldn't find the manila file under the piles of papers in the dining room. I had left a message earlier in the week, to ask about their interpretations of the drilling. While Tom finished the dishes and got the boys' hair shampooed, I initiated the conversation with who-knows-whom by stating that there seems to be a push for drilling without regard for the environmental consequences.

He replied, "There is undoubtedly money in the eyes of some people, but some of the companies are pulling back on leasing, due to the economy. There is less money available; loan money is drying up, but eventually it will be back."

He said that the Sierra Club did not want to be seen as naysayers in the drilling and that the goals of the Sierra Club were to protect the property—to try to limit surface and groundwater pollution, even on public lands. "We need to be sure that the company has made a proper agreement with the water treatment centers, that there are no local spills. What we fear is that the surface water could be damaged. The drill pads are off-road, so pollution could leach into streams, especially if the holding ponds are breached. We want to examine this from a management angle, making sure that things are done right, so that as little land as possible is compromised." He indicated that water warming in streams could lead to an increase in water pollution and, "Storm-water is mixed with sewage, and greater pollution ends in rivers. This will lead to increased phosphates in the sewage treatment plants. Water quality issues will arise in bays and oceans, where the water eventually appears.

Perhaps it was his willingness to explain the basic, larger environmental picture in a slow, step-wise manner that tipped me off that I was speaking with a professor—one who used the podium to untwist issues. I tried desperately to think of large words to employ.

We discussed the 'frack' water, which is pumped into the well to fracture the shale and release the gas, and I asked about water recycling, which I thought was possible.

Here, though, he veered into his political viewpoint. "Pennsylvania has a history of being ruled by the coal companies."

I grinned a little, inwardly, thinking that in southeastern Pennsylvania, near Philadelphia, where I was raised, no one I knew ever thought about coal and probably never had. In my graduate studies, I had learned about coal burning and associated mercury release and also about smog (a contraction of the words 'smoke' and 'fog'), which had led to deaths in the river valley of Donora, PA, in the 1940s and in foggy London, England, in the 1800s.

Coal mining seemed so linked to the past. I had studied human health issues, but not the field of economics, and thus had never seriously considered the connection between transporting fuel and cost: it is cheapest near the source. While searching for a house in the Appalachian mountains of Northeastern PA, I had stood, dumbfounded, when realtors glorified coal burning: "Coal is cheap and heats the house nicely. You only have to load up the furnace once a day."

Less than one hundred miles from New York City, people still shovel coal themselves! Even newer homes are often heated by coal, or a stove is kept as a back-up source of heat for the frequent winter power outages. So my education continues, though I haven't quite figured what a 'clinker' is.

The 'professor' continued, and my thoughts returned

from my scattered memories. "Landowners do not have the mineral rights under their land." I silently disagreed. We own our mineral rights, at the farm, and so does my mom in her house, downstate; however, I am learning that there are people in this region who do not. Those are the people who are the big losers in this gas-leasing game. Their own land surface can be destroyed but they have no way to stop the drilling, nor are they making money from the decimation. Our contractor told us as much about his own land; he was resigned to it.[1]

"The coal companies would follow a vein, destroy water supplies and yet not be liable," was his next comment. It sounded like an interesting lecture, but the loud splashing from the bathroom told me that I should not prolong the conversation. I propelled him to the present and told him my reasons for not wanting the gas extracted: besides the land being compacted by trucks, we don't know the long-term environmental and human health impacts. I asserted, despite the giggling in the bathroom, that we should focus on alternative energy sources rather than rely on coal or oil or even natural gas. He agreed, but indicated that there is a latency period until this can be done.

I mentioned that it didn't matter what I did; my

---

[1] In 2010, Tom and I went to a seminar on 'Tax Issues and Gas Leasing' as part of his continuing education. He learned that if the owner of the rights (such as a mining company) is no longer in existence (such as a defunct mining company), the mineral rights often revert back to the state under the 'Unclaimed Property' laws. Landowners may be able to reclaim them by contacting the state.

neighbors had already signed leases, and the gas was therefore destined to be extracted.

"I don't know that your neighbors will control your fate. You need to develop a relationship with them, to work with them to make sure things are done right. Try acting as a consultant, either paid or volunteer. It might be well received if they see it is in their own best interests … They might be suspicious of you, if they notice that your interest is in blocking the drilling. They don't want to lose the money. But perhaps you could convince them that they have a stake in seeing the groundwater protected."

When would I do this and how would I accomplish it? I am not so sure that I have time to work with my neighbors, to rally people who have already signed rights away with leases. It is too late, in my opinion.

He was very nice about my credentials, telling me that I should get them out, into this community, let people know who I am, and what my expertise is. He gave me the impression that there might be possibilities for me, career-wise, in the northeastern Pennsylvania area. That in itself was consoling. Now that I have a reviving interest, I am realizing that this sub region isn't a center for scientific research. I thanked him, hung up the phone, and hurried to towel off the boys and get them into bed. That half hour talk, though interesting, had eaten into my narrow window of 'Matthew-time.'

ço-ço-ço-ço-ço

The next day I called Jennifer Parker to ask about her hybrid car. Jennifer has a B.S. from Princeton and a PhD in chemical engineering from U.C.L.A. She is delightfully frank, and, about my 'eco-dilemma,' as she called it, she bluntly replied, "It would be 'just stupid' not to make money from something they are going to take, anyway. Your neighbors would be less likely to designate the money to environmental causes than you would. You cannot block the gas drilling; you should take the money. Designate a percentage—say, twenty percent—which would be sent up front to environmental causes."

I expressed my frustration about what the 'professor' I had spoken last night had said. "He suggested that I get my neighbors together. My neighbors have all individually signed their rights away. Perhaps later we could band up and oppose something such as pumping stations, but I have no time for that fight, not now, with a toddler. And anyway, these battles are not yet concrete. Not only do I not know what is going on in Wellsboro on a day-to-day basis, but I am an outsider, a flatlander."

Jennifer restated the position, adding, "Taking a stance alone will not matter. You are not in a position of strength. It is the same for Tom's plan to ask for a subsurface lease; they [the gas-leasing companies] have no reason to do it."

Her remark isn't quite optimistic, but perhaps is realistic. Discouraged, I decided that I didn't want to talk about it anymore. I asked about her life.

Jennifer told me that she loves her hybrid and revealed that she is studying anatomy so she can become a nurse.

"When do you have time to do that?" I asked, incredulous.

She laughed. "Stephanie, my children are in high school. I never see them before 6 p.m. During the day I have lots of time to kill."

I cannot imagine having time to kill and suddenly am not sure that I want to have it. Won't it be terribly lonely, without my little boys seeking my attention and love?

Halloween Nightmares

And Liberty plucks Justice by the nose,
The baby beats the nurse,
And quite athwart
Goes all decorum.

—William Shakespeare, *Measure for Measure*

October 30, 2008

Mom came to spend a day. The driveway was icy from a recent storm, and our telephone lines lay across the fence, but the sun was shining. Mom chatted with me and played with Michael while I sewed the tiger hood for his Halloween costume; then I called the car dealership on my emergency cell phone.

Last weekend, while our teenaged babysitter played with the boys at home, Tom and I test-drove two cars. The first was a hybrid. I like the prospect of getting fifty-five miles-per-gallon (mpg), and the car was all tidy and clean.

Still, I kept shaking my head. "It has so little trunk space."

"Oh," the dealer assured me, "The seats fold down."

I interrupted his attempt to highlight the feature of folding seats, teasing him, "It is likely illegal to drive with two children pinned under the backseat." The sport utility van, with lots more space, had the engine of a chipmunk, and didn't boast more than twenty mpg.

"No," was the response to today's call, "there is no zero percent financing for the hybrid." Suddenly there was no pressure to buy a car before tomorrow, the 31st, before zero percent financing disappeared. The car decision, thankfully, was shoved aside again. We could think about it for a while longer—a respite, considering Tom's job situation.

Mom helped me make meatballs and tomato gravy for dinner. Preparing this recipe is a ritual for me: picking fresh parsley and basil, chopping garlic and onions, and using tomatoes I have stored, frozen, from my garden. Mom uses tomatoes from a can and spices from the jar, yet hers always tastes better.

There never is enough time to visit, and she wants to get home before dark, so she can sleep in her own bed. I am afraid that is the way life will end, with us having snatched only small segments of time to visit and not really saying enough.

After Mom drove away, I put Michael to nap, and Matthew and I painted his green caterpillar Halloween costume. It was nice to be working together, though the fabric paints were messy and smelly. As the costume dried, I began an e-mail to Mike Gallo, but stopped to greet Tom as he appeared at the top of the steps, home from work.

Tom neglected his usual hearty welcome, pausing half-smirking as he looked from me to Matthew, who was on the floor surrounded by scraps of wet fabric. I furrowed my brow, confused, as he continued to stand in the doorway without offering any greeting. I can usually read his thoughts, but what is wrong? As I approached him, he abruptly blurted, "I've been let go from work."

Last February, when we first anticipated this likely development, I had considered it exciting to start afresh, to have a reason to relocate to an undefined 'somewhere else,' with new things to discover. Now a sudden sick feeling gripped my stomach. *Will we have to leave this house and our friends here?* Suddenly I was desperate to maintain the status quo.

I gulped and stared at him as we stood frozen in the doorway. I tucked my arm into his as he spoke dazedly, relaying details, "They want me to keep working until they transfer the business to the new owners."

I stood there dumbly, while Matthew demanded, "What's 'fired' mean?" over and over, an unheeded parrot in the background.

That night, Matthew's eyes were bothering him, again, and he panicked, thrashing around, crying, "Things are too big!"

He was distraught and we were frightened, not knowing what was wrong. We pulled him into bed with us for a while and finally tucked him back into his own bed, where he slept soundly. Neither Tom nor I did. We were trying to swim past the nightmarish foggy clouds of what might happen into some future certainty. It was, of course, an impossible endeavor.

October 31, 2008

This morning I got very little accomplished. Of all the ridiculous things, I sorted spools of thread! What a mindless waste of time; I hardly ever sew.

Michael wouldn't nap, but was adorable in his tiger outfit, racing about, "Me have a tail! Me have a tail!"

The phone service finally returned and it was if it had never been gone. How quickly I readjusted to that comfort, without appreciating the convenience. I made an appointment for Matthew to see a doctor this afternoon; it was an emergency, in my mind.

ജ‐ജ‐ഛ‐ഛ

Well, *what* a flabbergasting visit! That old doctor, not our usual one, claimed that Matthew was *imagining* the headaches! I asked him, (and I am so proud of my calmness) why he thought this to be so, and he replied, "Montessori children tend to be *different*!"

I blinked thrice and asked him what he meant by *different*.

"They are more imaginative because of their unstructured learning environment."

I gulped to maintain my composure then proceeded to quiz him about the possibility that it might be more serious, "We have never witnessed such a panic in him."

The doctor remained astonishingly indifferent. "The symptoms are innocuous."

The encounter gave me no satisfaction. I know when my child is concocting a story, and this man had the audacity to imply that I was not capable of reading my own child. I was angry that I had pulled Matthew out of school. It had been such a challenge, to get Michael to cooperate during the office visit. I had skipped lunch, myself, in order to get to the doctor's office on time, and then the doctor implied that my child was a liar.

When we got home, I put Michael in to nap. Matthew and I finished his costume. He seemed fine, now—no headaches or eye complaints. We sewed antennae and cut armholes and snipped off the bottom of an old sleeping bag, creating something from an old discard. It was fun to do crafts with Matthew, tired though I was. We ate early, before trick-or-treating, and I felt nervous exhaustion weighing heavily on me.

I had longed for a crisp, autumn evening of Halloween to walk along the dark roads with flashlights, shopping bags clutched in the hands of the kids who were all a-tizzy with anticipation. Tonight, with sloppy snow on the ground, Tom drove us to about eight houses while he waited in the car, not wanting to see the neighbors. How different things were turning out, much different than expected.

Calls

Let every man be quick to hear,
Slow to speak,
And slow to anger.

—James 1:19

November 5, 2008

Now that it appeared we might really need this gas-drilling money, I scoured the phone book for the number of the DEP, called, and spoke with a water quality specialist. He was open and well informed.

"Will you know if the gas companies drill horizontally?"

"They must fill out permits to do so," was his reply.

"Who is verifying where they drill?"

"The DEP oil and gas inspectors verify the work, and they are checking casings." I made a quick scribble, adding a question mark above the word, 'casing.'

"When they drill horizontally, they usually go Northwest and Southeast of where they have drilled vertically. Holes are there for a reason, and that is to intercept fractures. A couple of the places are using one drill pad and incorporating three well heads: one vertical to the monitor, the others horizontally, heading Northwest and Southeast. So it is possible to have one well site and drill in different directions."

I returned to the question mark about the casings and acknowledged my ignorance.

"There are multiple casings surrounding the bore hole," he explained, "and all are grouted in. This prevents corrosion and deterioration. They also add another layer of grouting through the water zone. They stop grouting at some depth."

There was a pause before he continued. "Keeping this industry in compliance on this matter is less of a challenge for us here at the DEP than usual. The gas drillers don't want water to leak into their boreholes, and we don't want the gas to leak out into the groundwater; therefore, we both want the casings for protection, if for opposite reasons. If it saved the industry money not to add an extra layer of casing, we would have to watch them more carefully—we'd have more to monitor—but here we have a mutual desire for a casing."

He mentioned that we should do a 'pre-drill' sampling of our water well.

"There is no requirement that the companies have to monitor the water wells, but there is a presumptive liability, should something go wrong. This means that the gas company would be financially responsible for drilling a new water well."

I smiled to myself and told him that we didn't have a well; our water was spring fed into a stone-lined pit about six feet deep. I told him that we didn't drink it. The water had been tested a few years back and found to have coliform bacteria, but we used it for cooking. He clearly did not like the idea of a surface well and was adamant that we should not even cook with the water. "I always tell people to get a well. I cannot emphasize enough that they should avoid a surface spring."

It would cost several thousand dollars to drill a water well, and Tom won't be game, not without the gas-leasing money. The water specialist mentioned that they have even seen surface wells contaminated by the gas drilling—artesian wells—where the water pressure is high underground.

I asked about radon. He explained that radon

concentration was linked more to geology than to hydrology. There are no high radon levels in the area he is responsible for testing.

How pleasant it was to be conversing on a scientific topic.

Next day, after lunch, Michael napped and I forced myself to do the thing I had been avoiding for two months: call the gas-lease man. My stomach lurched at the idea, but I agreed with Tom: if we were going to attempt to get a subsurface lease, we had to befriend this man. And if we were going to befriend the man, we had to do it this weekend, because we were closing the place for the winter. It was a bit late to be taking this step, I admitted to myself with a sigh, but nothing gets done on time these days.

In order to keep my thoughts in order and not tip him off about my hesitation to sign a lease, I made a list of questions in my little notebook:

Will you look over our site with us?

What is the overall plan, the big picture, for the Wellsboro area?

What direction will your company head in the future, when the natural gas is depleted and there must be is a change in energy sources? We need cleaner fuels.

I took a deep breath, let it out loudly, and dialed the number on the lease agreement. A male voice picked up right away. He sounded youthfully confident. My guess: mid-twenties. I was surprised; I had expected an older engineer.

I introduced myself and began to unleash my fabricated reasons for not getting back to him earlier about the gas-lease sent in August.

He quickly overrode my chatter. "The gas leases have come to a financial halt. We have stopped leasing and are focusing on drilling. We haven't caught up with our payments." I could tell he had repeated these lines over and over to many different callers. Clearly in haste to stem any request that I might make for money, he went on to say that we could void our lease. He explained that it is hard to get credit with the recent economic events—*no kidding*, I thought—and that things had changed. "It is taking longer to pay the signing bonuses."

I shifted the conversation, asking him questions about the drilling in Wellsboro. "We are drilling, and there is a pipeline, the Tennessee Gas Pipeline, north of town. We need to connect each well together. Near the Police Barracks, a landowner is allowing a transmission station to be built, only one of two compressor stations—they are expensive—in the whole Wellsboro area."

I had heard that the stations were loud, but didn't say anything. I asked about the wells near our house. "How far apart they were spaced?"

"Which wells?"

I told him, and he began to give me statistics, from his head or the computer, but with familiarity.

"It depends on the geology. They spread them forty acres apart at least. They don't want to tap into the same source or they won't get enough gas."

I asked how long the land would look like an industrial site.

He told me: "It looks like they will be building a house until the well has been online for about six months."

I raised my eyebrows but said nothing. That was some 'house'-building this summer.

"What's left is a 'Christmas Tree,' which is what we call the waist-high pipes and meters. That's all that's left."

You could farm on it, but you couldn't put a building on it. We ask the landowners about their plans," he added as an afterthought.

"Of course you do." I agreed sweetly, while venomous

doubts coursed through my mind. "So, uh, what are you drilling, horizontal or vertical wells?

"Some horizontal, some vertical, the cost is around one and a half to two million."

I spring-boarded from that comment to the information I really wanted. "That seems like a lot of money if you are only guessing where the gas is. How do you know where to look?"

"We are confident that our team of geologists and engineers can find it. The guys in the field find the formation underground by seismic testing. Those small explosions underground show us where to target. They send the geologist a spot on the map, and he petitions the state for permission to drill there. If the spot is not suitable, the state gets in contact with us. But," he cautioned confidentially, "We probably wouldn't put one on your land, even though you want it."

I hazarded a guess that now—when he had volunteered the information that all gas-leasing was at a halt—would be a good time to acknowledge that we did not want a well on our property. I asked if he would go over the site with us, because we weren't really interested in having our land damaged.

He told me that he wasn't on site, not in Wellsboro. Then he said that a non-surface clause is always a possibility. "Depends on how badly we want it leased."

The more he talked, the more information I gathered that might be used to my advantage. *Oh, why do I always chatter so? Listening always will get me so much more information.* I jotted notes furiously.

I asked about the next-door neighbor who had signed with a different gas company a few years ago.

"Well, they got their signing bonus; that's all. We may offer or sell leases to other gas companies in the area and the leases, if bought or sold, are honored and their terms upheld. We beat the competition there, but, being privately owned, we only make money when we drill and transport."

I wasn't quite sure what he meant or where he was going, but I kept probing. I wanted to know if they going under our land, already?

I asked about the drilling. It was so far underground. Did they know where they were drilling?

"It's an amazing computer video game. They know where they are."

"Could the gas be extracted from under our property by the new well?"

"Well, they wouldn't drill under your property, but I cannot say positively that all extraction is stopping at the property line. Getting the gas, well now, that's not an exact science."

"What does the company plan to do in forty years when the gas is gone?"

All his previous answers had been quick and well-honed, likely from repetition. To this question he did not respond immediately. "I'm not sure of the future. It's pretty clean energy." His words flowed smoothly again. "We'll need gas for transition."

There it was again. I'd heard it before: 'transition fuel.' The phrase implies, in my opinion, that we are all actively striving to alter our collective lifestyles. I don't seem to be making an effort toward 'transition.' Is anyone?

I thanked him for his time and he breezily replied, "You're welcome. Goodbye."

Closed for the Winter

November 7, 2008

At dawn I lay staring through the window at the creek mist rising across the road. I was coordinating, in my head, the logistics for the weekend. We planned to drive to Wellsboro in the afternoon, following Matthew's teacher conference, to close the place for the winter. I was immeasurably relieved that we would not be meeting with the gas-lease man and that we had a reprieve from the signing decision. *Maybe that bill will pass soon enough.*

Tom and Matthew left for work and school, and I packed for the short trip. We were only staying for two days, so it was reasonable to think that the task should be easily finished in a short time. I unplugged the computer, turned down the heat, watered the plants then headed to the living room, where Michael's toys were strewn everywhere. I grabbed some clothes for Michael.

As always, the kitchen was a mess of half-sorted objects. I couldn't find a lid to the water jug, and was scrounging among the pots and pans in the closet, when I came across a rotten onion. It took five minutes to wipe down that smelly shelf.

It seems as if every little chore around here takes five minutes: taking out the compost and the garbage, dressing Michael ... My life is punctured with five minutes jobs. No wonder I can't accomplish anything of larger significance.

I was making peanut butter and jelly sandwiches when Michael got tangled in the fishing line. He had started to play with the rods in the garage. After making a mess of the transparent string, he had tangled his feet and legs. It was hilarious to watch, of course, but another thing to repair. I finally decided to relocate outside with him. I'd disappear into the house, complete one chore, then hurriedly return.

The first time, I arrived to discover that he had emptied all twenty-five pounds of the most expensive birdseed onto the driveway. He proudly showed me that he could put its storage can in his wagon. On my hands and knees I tried to scrape some into a bucket to salvage for the goldfinches. Lately Tom has been eyeing my 'bird welfare,' as he calls it, as an unnecessary expenditure.

The last of the packing and cleaning always challenges me. I never say, "I am done," because I can always find one more envelope that needs a stamp, one more item that we might need to bring. The floors can always stand to be vacuumed. I wonder if my life will be frittered away on these tasks. At that thought I hurried outside to be with Michael. We were playing and watching when Tom drove up the driveway to change clothes and cars. I quickly buckled Michael into his car seat. We were off to Matthew's parent-teacher conference.

ৡৢৡৢ৶ৢ৶

I squeezed into the tiny chair the teacher offered across from her at the back table. She was especially formally attired today; I was especially not, since we were heading to the farm. She began by telling me how wonderful Matthew is as a student, and I beamed with pride. Then she tactfully revealed her concern that he was not progressing quickly enough in reading, and that occasionally he "spaces out" during class.

I hope there is nothing physically wrong with him. I 'space out' at times, too, when my mind is traveling down a thought sequence.

Well, nothing we can to do about it today. We will have

to be more attentive to his schoolwork in the future. We also agreed to having him evaluated by the school district.

I thanked her and we left the conference and drove to Wellsboro. When we arrive during daylight hours from spring to early fall, we always hurry from the car to 'discover' what is blooming, what fruit is setting, or how big the pumpkins have grown. Today no grapes dangled from the vines, no blueberries ripened to navy, nothing at all of summer. All was settling into dormancy, repose.

The warm wind rushed past my ears as we left the car, blowing the stuffiness and the busywork of the day from my thoughts. We walked to the top of our hill and the open fields. How relaxing to see sky for so many miles! Over the years, my view has been tarnished by a few houses, but it is still lovely, and the warmth of the air was a comforting blanket enveloping us. Its delightful breeze lured us into a comfortable, light-hearted ease; tricking us into forgetting about the cold blasts that were due to arrive.

Matthew began to fill Michael's little pockets, his baby blue hat, and even his own sock with thick yellow horse corn kernels that had spilled along the grassy track from the tractor leaving the neighbor's field. Tom and I stood in the moist breeze, scanning the scene of browns, purples and golds under the blue and deepening sky.

At dusk, we drove to town to get a bite to eat. First we stopped at the bookstore on Main Street, where I bought Christmas gifts and a hardback book for the boys; then guilt assailed me. I should be using the library for us, and do our nieces and nephews even read the books we buy for them? Buying books is an extravagance now that Tom has lost his job. We will soon possibly have no income.

The worried, hunted feeling followed me to the restaurant. *Should we order salads?*

"What? Three dollars for drinks for the kids? Get them water. We might have no income in two weeks."

Despite that unpleasant undercurrent, it was a good meal

in a cheery place. There is something about being surrounded with people, even strangers, when it is dark outside. There is comfort in human company when the days are growing shorter.

It was long past dark when we left and the air was still warm and smelled fragrantly of autumn as we retrieved the odd items from the backseat—a pair of boots, the coloring book. As Tom carried them into the house, he demanded, "Where is the bacon? Didn't you get it? You knew I wanted it!"

Since Halloween he has been cranky. I don't like the smell of bacon, but for once I did buy it for him.

"Did you look in the grocery bag?" I countered evenly, as I walked upstairs.

I made the beds, Matthew laid out pajamas and Tom swatted flies. Downstairs we snacked on pears and cinnamon bread with butter before hustling the boys back upstairs to brush their teeth. We read stories and said prayers. No one had dusted the baseboards, so our throats clogged from the dust rising from their warming tops.

৩৹৩৹৵৵৵

It is wonderful to be able to turn up the thermostat and take the chill out of the air in minutes. And yet, by installing the baseboard heat, we lost something—a slice of all the old memories. The memory is only one of being cold and uncomfortable, and yet, strangely, I don't want that feeling to be completely extinct.

In years past, when we opened the house on fall weekends, the damp indoor air would chill us to the bone. We swept floors and wiped counters while still bundled against the cold and never felt quite welcome until a fire was crackling in the hearth to banish the still hovering dank spirits. Although we carried our bags to the trapped warmth upstairs, unpacked our clothes and arranged the bedcovers, we would settle in near the fire downstairs to linger in the glow, to reacquaint ourselves with the place.

Long commutes and the work day eventually took their toll, and we yawningly conceded and wandered up to bed. The heat of the fire followed us up the first few steps and then dropped away; the air upstairs was now chilly in comparison. The fire snapped comfortingly as sentry for a few hours, but by dawn, it had died, and cold crept over us as if unfolding one cover at a time. When I finally awoke from a fitful sleep and forced myself to slip my head and arm from under the blankets, I would feel the chill full force. Pulling cold clothes onto a warm body takes courage, and my teeth would chatter as I hurriedly dressed.

I don't regret the decision to install the instant warming devices, but I am sad that the days are gone when we embraced a more primitive existence at the farm. The luxury of constant, easy indoor heat is a joy, but we survived without it for extended weekends and somehow the deprivation toughened us a bit, made us hardier. I am sad that my boys might know only coddled comfort.

৯৯৯৯

Saturday began warmish and breezy as Tom fried bacon for breakfast. While I waited to eat, I cleaned that awful fly dirt off the new window trim in the kitchen. I hate the fly dirt, and the specks remind me so much of all those years when I couldn't keep the house clean. It seemed an impossible task. We were only there on weekends, and we were busy with our careers. Every time we arrived we faced a repair to one of the houses or were mowing lawns or planting trees. Now, even with more free time and brand new window sashes, the fly specks return. Is there any way to get rid of flies or mice in a summer home?

After I finished breakfast, Tom helped me mount new coat hooks on the kitchen walls. They were handmade, forged iron hooks, from a blacksmith we had met in West Virginia. I purchased them this past year, when money seemed to be plentiful and I could easily afford the extravagance.

Will we still be able to buy such nice things? I wondered, as I turned to assist Matthew with his homework. We normally would have run straight outside to start a project, but today I was determined that we were going to take Matthew's education seriously. We were sitting at the table, struggling through a reading assignment, when Ray Statts arrived with a load of cow manure.

Ray lives down the road and cuts the hay from our fields to feed to his cattle. He doesn't pay us, but he mowed a path to the woods and agreed to bring a load of manure for our garden.

Tom, who—as I have mentioned—is rather surly these days, had remarked, "What guy is going to waste his Saturday morning hauling manure to your garden? He won't show."

However, Ray did remember and there was his dump truck. I rushed outside to direct the placement, promptly forgetting Matthew's homework.

Ray, who is only a part-time farmer, works for the town on their maintenance crew. He knows the community, and that is a nice 'in' for us to learn about local things. I mentioned that another farmer asked to use our fields for hog manure and offered to pay. The indignation over the 'factory' hog farms that have sprung up in the past few years around Wellsboro has yielded to the gas-drilling drama.

Ray looked at the ground and answered, "Well, now, he looks out for himself."

Ray didn't actually say something negative, but I got the point. The locals drop such subtly disparaging comments about one another now and then. I guess they have for generations. I know that I and other flatlanders forget that we are not as 'invisible' as we are in more populated areas. Here, the people you meet at church *are* the ones who you work with, and who you see at the high school football game. We are still learning that. Everyone knows everyone, they seem to be related to everyone else, and it is not safe to say anything that we don't want to have repeated to everyone. It certainly is playing with fire. I keep forgetting what a small community this is.

Ray changed the subject, becoming more animated as he described his draft horses.

"I was going to bring them to do the hay raking this summer, but you know the weather I was facing ... they're soft. If I worked them like the Amish do to their horses, they'd be able to do it."

We started in on the inevitable subject of the gas-leasing. Ray told us that he hadn't received his signing bonus yet, that the company had offered him a higher royalty percentage and only half of the signing payment instead. "That's where the big money is, in royalties," he asserted.

I could tell Tom was uncomfortable over our lack of a gas-lease. He kept kicking the grass with his boots, shifting his weight, and occasionally glowering at me.

Tom and I both like Ray. He is always straightforward about his plans for our fields, and it was very nice of him to remember to bring us the load of manure on his day off. We both noticed, however, that Ray did not reciprocate when I relayed the amount of our gas-lease offer. I petulantly mentioned that fact to Tom later.

He shrugged, "People here are tight-lipped about their business. It is a small community. You say something to one person and it gets around." I pursed my lips in a frown.

Matthew spread the composted manure on the tiny pine trees we had planted on the lawn, near the road, as a future buffer against traffic noise. Michael, meanwhile, grabbed two fishing poles from the front porch and tangled their lines. I feigned concentration on the manure, thus forcing Tom to notice Michael's antics and untwist the lines while I dumped shovelfuls onto the rhubarb bed that runs the length of the east side of the house. Mrs. Penney must have started it over fifty years ago, for it was already an enormous patch when we arrived on the scene. My sister and I would have sword fights with the stalks, laughing as we gouged each other's shield of giant rhubarb leaves.

I sent Matthew to get the little red wheelbarrow. Michael, a stocky little figure in his baby blue hat, trundled after him. They were gone quite awhile, and eventually I hurried up the hill to search for them, worried that they had hurt themselves amongst all of the junk in the barn. I found them walking along the path from the field and pushing the little barrow, filled with yellow horse corn kernels. It was so adorably cute to see them together. Michael, his face red with cold and alight with joy, came running and leapt into my arms. It was a perfect moment and a lovely memory: my boys had been diligently 'working' in the cold air; they were not the lazy victims of soft comforts.

Inside the warm house, we dumped coats and hats onto the chairs, ignoring the new hooks we had screwed into the wall this morning. We washed our stiff hands under warm water and then we tried to nap. Tom left to go golfing.

When I rose an hour later, I noticed that the temperature, inside and out, had dropped further. I couldn't get warm, so Matthew and I had licorice tea and talked—a much needed cuddly time. When he started to examine the contents of the toy box, I began to pack up the food stored in the kitchen cabinets and brought in porch furniture for the winter. When Michael awoke, he offered to help move his tiny bench inside. We continued with the outdoor chores after Tom returned. My back was soon stiffer and Michael's hands were colder.

Sue Owlett, the attorney's wife, pulled her truck off to

one side and sauntered across the lawn, her beautiful blond hair swinging in a ponytail behind her. Sue has an inner calmness that I attribute to country living, as trite as that may sound. Since relocating from a metropolitan area, my life has decelerated to such an extent that I can, upon arriving in the even more rural Wellsboro, immediately recognize tourists by their energy levels.

Tourists are wired; they stand out not only because of their obvious disorientation, but in Wellsboro, because of their jumpiness. A vacation can open the mind, extend horizons, and all that good rot, but one thing it cannot do is allow the tourist to internalize the pace of a place. I can take photos and buy souvenirs, commit to memory the rhythm of life, but I can't bring that cadence home.

At the farm, I am more at peace, and I silently resolve to remain so, a resolution that is immediately obliterated by re-entry into fast-moving traffic

Sue smiled and raised a hand in greeting. When in earshot, she inevitably began talking about the gas leases.

"Did you sign?" she asked. Evidently, she had not heard that the leases were being retracted.

"Not yet." Tom replied.

I commented about my lack of interest in promoting global warming.

"You drive a car," she said, as she swung her slender arm wide to point at our driveway.

Once again, I felt that my position was not easily explained, especially in a one line quip. I have not boiled down all of my confusion into simple sentences and phrases, and, in general, I don't think quickly enough for conversation. I mumbled something about promoting alternative fuels.

"I can't even get windmills approved in the middle of nowhere," she burst out, "at the sawmill. There is nobody for miles!" I knew that her mother's family owned a lumberyard in town, and I think her dad used to oversee a lumber mill farther west, so that must be the connection.

I mentioned that we were surprised so few people consulted an attorney about their lease agreements.

She heartily agreed, "People don't use lawyers here ... Our neighbors call us at night, asking if they can bring the lease over."

"They are intimidated by the office setting," I said.

She shrugged. "My husband has them come over. They are neighbors. What are you going to do?"

Tom said, "Tell him we'll be over tonight."

We all laughed, and I hastily tried to clarify my thoughts on the matter. I hated tossing an idea out, having it beaten down with one swipe, and then standing there, misunderstood, unable to articulate my concerns. "Even though I am a hypocrite," I began, and Sue laughed again, "I think it would be better to set up solar panels and wind turbines than gas derricks."

Sue swept her arm again, this time dismissively. "They are predicting an enormous amount of gas out of each well. Behind our house, a simple calculation would say that the well would yield $200,000 a year. *A year!* That is an enormous amount. It galls me that I can see, from my own house, a derrick, and none of that money is going to us, all because of where they set up the lines to determine who gets the shares. We weren't pooled into that well. And we have three kids to get through college!"

I asked about their oldest son and his college plans. Tom's boots were churning the tufts of grass again and he looked away from me.

"He got an 800 on the math SATs," she smiled. "He's thinking about Princeton or Tufts."

The conversation veered to financing college, with Sue contributing, "I'm in charge of investments in our family."

"I hide my money in the mattress," I countered, jesting.

She replied, seriously. "When the people who bought that old trailer we found on the property paid us, they brought money in glass-jars—*cash*—and the jars were *cold!* They kept their money in the freezer. They told me that money doesn't burn in the freezer."

Michael interrupted by running over, barefoot. I swept him up into my arms, exclaiming, "Baby, you need shoes on your piggies!"

Sue excused herself, her long ponytail streaming behind as she departed. As I carried my little boy back to the porch, it occurred to me that I still hadn't articulated my thoughts as well as I wished. At least I'd spoken coherently, and anyway, conversations never travel in direct paths.

The boys went into the house to get warm, and Tom and I walked to the barn with geese honking overhead. White tufts of milkweed down, soft to the touch, dangled from dead, bleached hollow stalks in the hayfield. We closed the barn doors and secured the latch.

After dinner, I did the dishes while the rest showered; then we had a fire and popcorn. After we snuggled the boys in bed, Tom and I went downstairs to sit in front of the stone fireplace. I was staring at it, wondering how we could clean its catalytic converter, when Tom interrupted my thoughts and dragged me into a discussion about the gas-lease. I sighed to myself, and round and round we went, as usual. Tom said that he had already missed out on the money, and now he was out of a job.

I contradicted him. "No, the neighbors accepted their offers earlier this summer, and they still haven't received their money. We were later in the queue. Sue Owlett told us they had been knocking on doors all summer and you know they couldn't find us very easily. Remember? They had to mail us a lease."

That night neither of us slept well. Where would we be, now that Tom's job would soon be gone? Should we move to someplace cheaper, or back to New Jersey, where he could find work? Could I take that pace again? Should I sign the lease, so we could live in a slower place or, if we moved to a crowded area, be able to afford the amenities that would buffer the pace? Sue Owlett said $200,000. I would be a fool not to take it.

೫೨೪೪

Michael woke everyone early the next morning. The easiest routine was to clean each room and then leave it. Tom took the boys downstairs to get cereal, and I stripped the beds and covered them with giant plastic sheets for the winter. The new recently upstairs bedroom provokes the admiration of visitors, and I rather resent their enthusiasm, though I'm not quite sure why. I, too, love the polished wooden flooring, the openness, and the brightness from the big windows. It is cheerful, but I cannot help thinking it is somehow disrespectful to the old part of the house—the part that supports this room and has stood the test of time. Maybe it is that this room represents modern life: we now create spacious indoor places because we spend so little time outdoors.

But no matter the reason, the views from the new bedroom are wonderful, and I paused from jamming pillows into the old trunk to gaze out the east window, where the glowing sun rose into shiny, steel-blue clouds. The morning light created burgundy purples in the wood copse on the side of the barn and in the big, southern-facing window, the surprisingly bright, cream-colored stalks in the neighbor's cornfield attracted my attention.

Perched alone in the field on the distant hill, an old field barn is now collapsing. Years ago, when Tom and I re-roofed the back side of this house, that barn was lovely. *Ten years ago … What a lot has happened in ten years!*

I was writing my thesis that autumn, but had willingly

put aside the writing to do physical labor at my farm. Pausing to rest on sticky asphalt shingles, I had looked across the fields, wistfully wishing for a permanent chance to see this aerial view. We never really imagined that we would have this addition, on the very spot where I had sat. What delightful views and what other nice additions to our lives have arrived since then. But ten years have wreaked havoc on the field barn; it was a heap now.

৩০-৩০-৩৬

Downstairs, the boys wrestled and I ate breakfast while Tom began to carry things to the car. There really wasn't that much to do, and packing is rather a routine. We hadn't been here for very long, so the clutter on the kitchen countertop was minimal.

Before leaving we walked up to the cornfield. Matthew wished to collect more horse corn to feed the chipmunks at home. The grasses were burnt orange and brown. I tried to enjoy the loveliness of the view, but with my shoulders hunched to protect my shivering back, I could only think of seeking shelter. The cold wind driving through my clothing blew away my enthusiasm. I hurried Matthew in his task.

I didn't gather more marjoram from the kitchen garden, and I didn't take the time to look at the back flower bed. With the boys already in the car, Tom waited on the porch while I finished locking the doors.

I walked over to the old, green apple tree by the well house, thinking of all of the times Dad and I had picked apples there before leaving for home. I pulled five of them from the lower branches before returning to Tom. "Every time I leave here," I said wistfully, "I get farther away from Dad."

"You are actually getting closer to him, every day," he remarked, with quiet humor. My aching back agrees.

Odds and Ends

As soon as you trust yourself, you will know how to live.

—Johann Wolfgang Goethe

November 20, 2008

On the news I thought I heard that DEP asked for more staff to monitor gas drilling, but the boys were hollering and running through the kitchen, so I wasn't able to get any details. Well, hiring more staff would be a step forward.

We need to decide where we can earn enough money to live. Tom needs access to clients who are affluent. I do not want to give up the backyard hemlocks or the rhododendron leaves that curl when it is cold. They are here, but, or maybe because they are, job opportunities are not.

The notes from one of my journals are all typed into my 'manuscript.' I need to start the next journal if I am going to write this for publication. I am glad, though, that I spent much of this evening lying in bed next to Matthew, listening to an account of 'his day' before he went to sleep. I want to hear his thoughts, and tonight he was quite talkative. I think his stress of homework, piano, and doctor's appointments has decreased.

Earlier in the week, I took him for a routine checkup and was surprised when three interns followed our pediatrician into the tiny room. She provided brief introductions.

Matthew was clearly discomfited by so many strangers, not to mention the doctor, the nurse, Michael and me—all of us staring at him. As the doctor began to examine him, I mentioned that he was having trouble reading. Matthew wouldn't respond to any of the doctor's questions, and he curled up, shirtless, in the cold room. Certainly the doctor viewed him as a child who was avoiding interactions with adults, for she labeled him as having Attention Deficit Disorder and suggested that we start him on pills. She and her entourage exited in a long line as I stared at the prescription.

Lying in bed with me in the dark, Matthew told me about his day. I am glad that I now know that his friend John wasn't allowed out for recess because of his poor health, and that made Matthew lonely. I cuddled him and he told me that he knew they hadn't really walked two miles in gym class—as another boy had claimed—and that 'octopus and fish' was a fun game with the same rules as 'sharks and fishes.' We both marveled that the man who visited their class took seven years to write his first book. I confided that I would like to write a book, but that I didn't want to wait seven years. That that was as long as Matthew had lived, he reminded me!

I now see my boy as I used to, as a joyful little creature full of potential, whose observations and chatter are worth hearing.

Christmas Film Festival

A good conscience is a continual Christmas.

—Benjamin Franklin

December 30, 2008

We spent a week with Tom's family at Christmas and enjoyed all the excitement that abounds when Santa Claus is on his way. Washing dishes in the kitchen after the enormous dinner, Scott, my brother-in-law, talked to me about his recent trips to Asia. I am fascinated by his observations, but he is exhausted from the travel.

Of course for us, the gas-leasing issue has receded for now, but according to the Web pages of the Penn State experts, the leasing and drilling will ramp up again in the future.

I still wanted to hear Scott's perspective, which was connected to his knowledge of industry. "It doesn't matter what you do; the actions of the Chinese are overwhelming the system. Not extracting your minute amount of gas won't make a difference." He, like my own brother, professes that technology will be the means of saving our resources.

I frowned, despite the hubbub and general gaiety surrounding me. He might be speaking truth, but I think that we should maximize our own attempts to preserve the planet. Shouldn't we begin to implement other helpful strategies, and sooner rather than later? But which ones? Which will have the most impact? I thought again about looking this up, but the dishes were piled and little children were racing around unimpeded amidst the expensive porcelain figurines in the living room.

ॐॐॐॐ

I spent one late evening with Madeline and Rex at their home. Tom encouraged me to get out for a bit of fun, and it was a relief to converse without the boys running around to distract me. Of all of our 'couple' friends, Rex and Madeline seem to be the ones who cherish each other the most. Each is considerate of the other, never revealing anything but the best. Rex remarked that the way I had sketched the natural gas scene in my holiday letter had illustrated the disharmony that exists between Tom and me. I felt subdued. I had intended my account to be humorous.

Rex, en route to the kitchen for tea, mentioned a movie about the Teapot Dome scandal, the turn-of-the-century oil monopoly that I vaguely recall from tenth-grade American history class. "They made a movie about the extraction of the neighbors' oil."

I blinked. I didn't know that. *Where have I been?* I wondered.

We took our tea into their dining room and Rex folded his fingers around his mug, cocking his head to one side as we discussed the issue. "In the future, you could convince your neighbors not to join in, to resist," I muffled a snort as he finished, "but that isn't likely." He shook his head slowly and gripped his cup more tightly.

"The problem I have," he went on, shifting in his seat, "is that, where the rubber hits the road, you may keep your principles, but that you will be ineffective in changing anything."

I agreed, and quickly asserted, "More than anything, I think that at this stage of our lives we want to be effective."

We discussed how to make oneself effective in any situation. We agreed that our worlds had expanded since the old college days, that we now have more potential to have a positive impact on a larger scale. As to this immediate situation, Rex thought it might be best to, "Get into bed with them to change them."

I furrowed my brow, repulsed by the idea, which has a deceptive ring to it, at best.

I mentioned that I wanted to write about it, to publish the story. Madeline said that it might have some movie potential. The two of them amused themselves by concocting a storyline while I nibbled a slice of pumpkin bread. I suppose dreaming up movie plots has some entertainment value.

"It needs a twist—the leads should need the money," Madeline asserted.

Rex chimed in, "The poor farmer contracts cancer … Let see …" He slapped his palm on the table, "and it's caused by fossil fuel pollution!"

Madeline picked up the storyline, "The neighbor's gas well spilled contaminants into the water and caused this disease."

Rex finished triumphantly, "He doesn't have insurance and will have to sign a gas lease in order to pay for the treatments!"

They both seemed so tickled by their creation. I gaped at them for a moment, my snack balanced mid-air on my fork. Having spent the last four months in mental turmoil, I was stunned at this tangential, light-hearted spin on the story.

The next day Madeline rode to the mall with me so I could return a gift. "It's nice to spend a few minutes alone," she said. "Rex has been annoying me lately. He always seems to dominate the conversations."

My jaw dropped, but I managed to keep my eyes on the

road ahead. I had believed their marriage to be as close to ideal as possible. Despite my shock, it was oddly comforting to learn that even their marriage had defects.

Unequal Vision

February 17, 2009

Matthew has been diagnosed with a 'coding' problem—something about his eyes not being able to translate for his mind the material that is on a written page.

Early in December I met with the school district's psychologist and his teacher. When the former paused to glance at her papers, I, recalling the doctor's diagnosis, asked if Matthew could have Attention Deficit Disorder.

The teacher intercepted my question. "Matthew is a hardworking, quiet student who is not disruptive in any way." She leaned forward and enunciated each syllable slowly and distinctly, as if I was hard of hearing, "This is a Read-ing Prob-lem, Mrs. Hamel."

"Just asking," I said, tilting my head and smiling brightly. The psychologist went on to discuss test results, 'phenomic awareness' and other only vaguely comprehensible education words to me.

Matthew could transfer immediately into the public school, where he could get additional learning support, but Tom and I rejected that option. It did not seem profitable to yank our sensitive little son from his school and stick him mid-semester into one that is seven times larger. If next fall there is still a problem, we will transfer him.

I took him to see another eye doctor. According to tests, Matthew's eyes are not tracking properly and he has poor depth perception. At first I wondered if this eye doctor was a quack; the optometrist last year had not noted any problem and, furthermore, had indicated that Matthew's acuity was superb. However, the eye issues are apparently unrelated to acuity. The diagnosis rang true. For months, Matthew had been 'sounding out' words that didn't make sense.

"Cawh? Why did you make the 'wh' sound, Matthew? There is no 'wh' in cake."

His left eye was reading one line, his right, the one below. Now he goes to occupational therapy twice a week. Already we are noticing improvements in his hand/eye coordination. It is strange and good to notice subtle progress in areas where we had never perceived deficiencies. Matthew works with therapists who use specially designed computer programs, while I chase Michael around the halls of the clinic.

Dr. Hamel, I Presume

February 27, 2009

I had checked out a new release from the library, knowing that I wouldn't read it, but acknowledging that I should read it. I never read anything scientific from the public library, don't ask me why. I never get further than bringing it home. It doesn't cost me a penny to check a book out of the library, and hope springs eternal, I guess.

This week's book was on the topic of Peak Oil and the end of fossil fuel usage. The book reminded me of the editorial in the newspaper: we are at the peak of oil production and will not be able to depend on cheap hydrocarbon fuel sources for long.

Tom picked the book from my pile in the living room and became engrossed. An hour later, he leaned over, tapping his hand on the page: "The Pentagon is planning to be off fossil fuels by 2050." I looked up from writing in my diary, as he continued solemnly, "We must alter our lifestyle."

I grinned to think that Tom had become a convert.

One evening a week later, I found Tom on the couch reading my manuscript. It bothered me that he would be judging my poor writing, so after he fell asleep on the bed with Michael, I snatched it to hide it. Instead, I began to read. After a few pages, I sat farther back on the couch. This wasn't bad. It clearly has holes in it—big holes—but it had some interesting dialogue.

I phoned the university staff last week to ask if they had any information on how to protect my property in the future, when the gas-leasing returns. I had found the number on their website then scribbled it onto the manila folder containing the notes I'd made during gas-lease conversations last fall. A nice young woman recommended a person to contact—Bob Ehrlenmeyer* of the Cooperative Extension— just as Michael began to yank the telephone cord and screech with annoyance. How far I have regressed from being professional!

Today I recalled my intention to telephone Mr. Ehrlenmeyer. I have learned that there is no reasonable way to hold a conversation while Michael is racing around unchecked, so I let him watch a movie, detesting that I was doing so. I have little tolerance for setting children in front of a screen; yet here I was doing it again, just like last week when I first called his office.

His assistant had said to call this morning. When Mr. Ehrlenmeyer again wasn't available I began to wonder if he was screening a deluge of landowner calls.

"Well, perhaps I could give you my name, and you could ask him to call me."

"Yes, that would be fine," she said. "What is your name?"

I paused. In academic circles, it is considered inappropriate to 'brag' about your degrees. Unlike medical doctors, who use their title everywhere, a PhD does not universally use 'Doctor' as a title. If Ehrlenmeyer was a professor or, worse yet, a professor emeritus, my proclaiming myself to be 'Dr.' Hamel would be a gaff—rather like smugly introducing myself as 'The Duchess,' only to learn that I was so condescendingly speaking to 'The Queen'.

Still, during these months of searching for answers, I have usually possessed only a vague understanding of who was on the other end of the telephone line. One thing is distressing clear: I have a sad bias of assuming that every man I speak with is a professor, *not* a secretary. There is more confusion when speaking to women. It is better, I have decided, for a woman to err on the side of bragging. They know even less about you than you do about them!

"Dr. Stephanie Hamel." I replied crisply. "Please ask him to call me this morning, or tomorrow morning. I am not in during the afternoon. Thank you." Somehow, the authority in my voice didn't convey the fact that "being in" meant I was in sweatpants and cleaning the house, tending to the incessant demands of a two-year-old. It sounded professional.

He'll call me, I know. He might think I am obnoxious, but he'll call me.

Michael's movie ended, so I read him a few stories as we lay down to nap. He was asleep, and I had rested, when the phone rang. I let it ring three times. It was Ehrlenmeyer. I had heard his remarks on a taped forum a few months back and recognized the voice.

I began my slightly rehearsed speech. "Thank you for returning my call. I have three questions that I was hoping you could answer. Is this a good time to give me a few minutes?"

He assented, so I described my academic career, briefly adding, "That background isn't important for this conversation, but it does influence me and is the reason I do not want to sign a gas-lease in the future. So, my first question is," and I read from my notes, "even though it is illegal to drill under land that is not leased, could the law possibly be enforced?"

I was on a roll, so I impulsively added question number two, "By not leasing, am I tempting them to drill close to my property so they can get things via, hmm, what is that word?" I fumbled, knowing it started with a 'c,' but forgetting anything else.

"Law of Capture."

"Yes, yes! That's it, the Capture Law." I felt like a dunce.

Mr. Ehrlenmeyer's response indicated that he was well versed on the subject and had repeated his answers often. "My read on the short term is that they wouldn't try to drill on the property line. Lease men come door-to-door and say that the companies will drill and capture the gas, but that isn't happening, not typically.

"In theory," he continued, "the gas companies could be doing this. In technical terms, it isn't happening. This shale is dense, and the gas isn't seeping over long distances."

His comments confirmed what I had read.

"They can fracture the shale with explosives," he went on, " 'fracking' it, to release gas."

He asked two rhetorical questions, "Can the exploration extend under unleased property? Is that trespassing?"

I interrupted to ask, "How far does it 'frack'?"

"Well, in theory, they could go about a thousand feet, but these wells are not draining far. Most engineers are saying that they drain several hundred, maybe five hundred feet. Is it likely that they are coming up to the edge of properties, drilling and 'fracking'?"

He answered his own question, "I have seen many plats, and the companies seem to be leaving a lot of space between the bottoms of the wells, of the hole." He had used an unfamiliar term—'plats'—which I think meant maps of the drilling. I was a little confused about leaving space between the bottoms of the wells; I think he meant the horizontal distance between two wells.

"The energy companies are not in it to get sued. There are differences of legal opinion within the industry as to whether or not 'fracking' under non-leased land is considered trespassing."

I asked how they would make that decision.

"It could be decided, legally, in another state."

I thought of Tennessee, or West Virginia, where these companies originate, or Texas, where they have been drilling the Barnett Shale for twenty years. Pennsylvania is new to this game.

"That is a reason why these companies are leaving a buffer between the bottom holes of these wells."

"Well, getting back to my question," I said, "how can I ensure that they don't do this?"

"There is no way of proving it; it can't be watched from above ground. The landowner has the responsibility of proving that the gas company has drilled under the land or 'fracked' it."

"There is no way I can do that." I stated, dully.

"No, there is not," he agreed.

That stunted my questions. His answer deadened my thoughts for a few moments. I hesitated but, realizing that my time was limited, plunged into my manuscript idea. "Finally … I was wondering … uh, I don't have an interest in writing about the science here, but do you know of anyone who would be interested in publishing some essays on the emotional and ethical considerations of gas-leasing?" I hurriedly added, "I think that there were a lot of people, like me, who initially said, 'No,' but realize that the money could be used in other ways to benefit the world and the environment."

He thought a moment. I do respect people who can think before speaking. I usually blurt out the first thing that comes to mind. I was wishing I had that restraint, when he replied, "I think this would be for the mainstream media."

I was immediately discouraged, thinking he was dismissing my idea and thus dropping me over a tall waterfall, with lots of rocks at the bottom. However, he continued, as if he was really contemplating my idea seriously. "You are suggesting that there is a middle ground, a segment of people who are conflicted about how to proceed—whether or not to lease their land."

"I would emphasize the emotional turmoil," I said. "When I watched that cable special, I noticed that there was a wide variety of people there, both in the forum and in the audience, with different outlooks on the subject. But more so, even within my own marriage, I judge the gas-drilling and consequent fossil fuel burning harshly, while my husband regards it as a way to early retirement."

I could hear the amusement in his voice when he replied, "Do you know about PASA?" I did know. It is a Pennsylvania organization that promotes sustainable agriculture. My post-doctoral advisor at Rutgers had gone to their meetings.

"About a month ago, one current member took the money," he went on. "I don't know if the well was on his property or an adjacent one, but he used his new found wealth from under the surface to implement some more sustainable agriculture approaches above the surface."

Mr. Ehrlenmeyer then indicated that he, himself, might be interested in reading something on the more human side of it. I was grateful for his encouragement, even if he was simply being polite.

"Well, it will be several months until I complete the manuscript, but I will send you something." I thanked him for doing all that he was doing, and wished him a good day.

It is difficult to find the time to write. With Matthew's school intensity, it will be a struggle, especially with Tom working so hard. He is still working for his old employer as an outside contractor and also trying to finish a few tax returns at night. I sighed and drove to pick up Matthew for piano lessons, with Michael messily eating his peanut butter and jam sandwich in the backseat.

Fragrant Spring

If you can taste the fruit before it
blossoms,
you've found faith, faith and so much
more.

—David M. Bailey, "So Much More"

April 21, 2009

A few days from early spring come to mind, especially that
fresh sunny day that I wasted while anxiously trying to
decide whether to buy a new car.

Spring meant warmer weather, which meant more gas
fumes in my car. Something had to be done. I was flip-
flopping on whether to buy a hybrid or buy a less expensive
car with pretty good gas mileage. Tom voted for the latter,
which is the size of the car I own already. If I wasn't getting a
hybrid, I wanted something bigger for my growing boys.

Still, this winter Tom had been following me around the
house, monthly credit card bill in hand, reciting the grand
total of our expenses. I found this information entirely
useless; I would ask him to isolate where we could do better,
instead, so I could try to cut back. Instead, he would list the
amount of the rent, the insurance, the food bills, the 'fixed
costs.' I indicated the things I would not cut, namely, organic
food. It was a circular process that offered no resolutions.

So, on that spring afternoon, I lay with Michael while he

settled for his nap, my head aching from calls with car dealers and arguments over money. As I rested, I realized that I would rather keep my old car than try to negotiate with car salesmen. If we stopped "needing" a new car, but instead fixed the gas tank of the old one, we would lose a smaller lump of money from our bank account.

During that short interval of time, while I lay with Michael agonizing over the decision, a surprising thing happened: I suddenly stopped caring what anybody else thought of my car. For me a car should serve a functional purpose only. The realization was freeing, and rather shocking, as well; I hadn't thought of myself as having shallow concerns about the world's opinion of my car.

I called our new mechanic and started to make arrangements. According to him, a new gas tank would cost $1,500, which we would have to supply up front, if they could find one to purchase. Also they were reluctant to yank the old one, not knowing what else might rain down on them in the rusty shower created by their dismantling.

So, when the mechanic called the next week to tell me that there were three gas tanks that would work for our car left in the country, he proposed replacing the tank's plastic overflow before purchasing the gas tank. I reminded him that the dealer had done so after the car had been damaged when Michael was a baby. One autumn day while we were at the park, a neighbor had backed into the back side panel. Soon after the body repair work was finished, the fume smells had erupted and I had taken it to the dealer, who had replaced the overflow. Still, the smell had resurfaced the following spring, so I was willing to let him try it.

The first afternoon that the car was at the shop, the mechanic phoned to tell me that when they were replacing the overflow, they noticed that the gas cap was cracked and so had replaced that as well. Would I try the car for a few days, in case the cracked gas cap had been causing the problem with the leaking fumes?

Why hadn't I thought to look at the cap? I never see it, that is why. In New Jersey, motorists do not pump gas, attendants do, it is the law. When we moved to Pennsylvania, I kept paying to have gas pumped. It was a luxury we could afford, and I convinced myself that since I was pregnant and wanted to minimize solvent exposure, it was the right thing to do. I seem to have been conveniently able to ignore that I am no longer pregnant.

And so, the fume problem appears to be gone—problem solved—for less than thirty dollars. I shiver to think I might have replaced my entire gas tank, or the car, because of a broken gas cap.

After picking up my old Subaru with its new gas cap, I drove through a muddy lane near home. I had arranged to pick up some scrap wood from a construction site to build the boys a sandbox. The builder was glad that I could use the wood; it would have been burnt otherwise. The boys helped me choose from the fresh smelling lumber, and we piled it into the trunk of my old car. I wouldn't have done that with a new hybrid, and the new sandbox cost me only the price of the sand and a batch of chocolate chip cookies, which I delivered the next day. It prevented some wood from being burned—temporarily, at least.

On another fine spring day when Mom arrived to visit, Matthew was hammering the pieces together. He cheerfully continued to pound, creating his own sandbox, while I listened rather sadly to Mom's recounting of Aunt Betty's fall. Was it a stroke? Why was there need for brain surgery to remove a blood clot? Why is Aunt Betty, once a vivid soul, reduced to existing in a hospital bed? How can the nurses know her ability to tell hilarious stories, her funny intonations, her kindness and her laughter?

While Mom sorrowfully spoke of Aunt Betty, she handed me a splash of glowing yellow with a few hyacinths added for fragrance. Oh, spring! When the daffodils are blooming, you *are* here. Matthew barged in to show her his handiwork, and so our thoughts were dragged from the sad lost ones back into our present, lively existence. Life must be grabbed on the fly.

Compromises

Ideals are like stars; you will not succeed
in touching them in your hands. But, like
the sea-faring man on the ocean desert of
water, you choose them as your guides,
and following them, you will reach your
destiny.

—Carl Schurz

Madeline's voice sounded desperate. It was a September
afternoon, and I had been staring into the refrigerator,
hoping for divine inspiration about what to serve for dinner,
when the phone rang.

"What's up?" I asked, closing the door. Sometimes
prolonging the dinner decision helps.

"Rex's mom just called. They have been discussing the
gas-leasing up there with her sister."

"Oh, I hadn't heard that leasing was back yet," I said. Not
that I had been following the natural gas news; I preferred to
ignore the subject.

"Well, it seems that the whole community is being
offered leases—a one-time deal. They have set aside the fire
hall for signing, this afternoon and tomorrow."

"That seems odd. Is it a meeting to get advice, like from
Penn State?"

"No, this is a signing meeting. She thinks she wants to do
it, since everyone around her is. But Aunt Catherine* is
against it." Aunt Catherine is a New York City inhabitant
who definitely has the 'flatlander-save-the-beauty-of-the-
country' mindset.

"Well, has an attorney looked over the lease?"

"No, that's just it. The company wants them all to sign now. I keep worrying about the water. What if her well gets ruined like in Dimmock?"

"Madeline, I think it's a bad idea to sign anything without having your own attorney view it. She could be handing over rights she doesn't know she has. She needs addendums added that will be in her favor, when the lease is renegotiated, down the line. *The Penn State Landowners' Guide* can tell her better than I can. I will photocopy a copy and drop it off to you. I'll give you our attorney's address and she can call him. I trust him implicitly, but if she would prefer someone local, he likely could recommend someone. "

I glanced into the living room, where Tom was tossing a tennis ball into the air, practicing his serve without a racquet.

"By the way," I asked, "How much are they offering?"

"$6,700 per acre." I gulped. This was a staggering amount. It made my $2,500 per acre look paltry in comparison.

The leasing dollars were high, by Pennsylvania standards, because they were near gas pipelines to New York City. There are ancient geological factors, as well, but regardless, prices in Wellsboro would soon be high, too. In ten years, or two cycles of leases, we would be passing up—even at $5,000 an acre—a half million dollars! I scratched the surface of the stove with my fingernail and sighed into the phone as we said goodbye. I knew what Tom's reaction would be.

And so it was. Tom's face, when I told him the amount, was blank. He simply stared at me, without saying a word. Dinner conversation, like the food, was not particularly enjoyable that evening. The empty silences and coldness that had pervaded our home last September had returned, cloaking us in misery.

Could I really expect Tom to forgive my passing up *that much* easy money?

A week later, I broke the stalemate and quietly sat down next to him. "Well, let's get back to what we said at the beginning. I can't allow drilling on the land, but I can allow you to ask for a subsurface lease for the gas under it. I suggest that we compromise."

"I don't think that is much of a compromise."

I stared a moment and then spluttered indignantly, "Why, it is an *enormous* compromise! I just sacrificed my environmental principles, something I do *not* want to do! *How* can you not call that a sacrifice?"

"Because they won't go for it, that's why. This is theoretical. They won't go for it, and we won't get any money."

I took a deep breath and sighed it all out. "Well, I want you to have the money if you want it. If anyone can negotiate it, you can. You are very persuasive and persistent." Tom softened a bit at my words. I could see that he was pleased, though I am not sure if it was because I had faith in him or if he had permission to negotiate for some dollars.

Tying Up the Leases

The next day, with his characteristic tenacity, I heard Tom joking on the telephone with a gas drilling company representative. Give this man a job and he sinks his teeth into it immediately. I grinned inwardly, despite my dislike of the compromise.

First, Tom wouldn't accept the comment by the gas-lease guy that they wouldn't sign a subsurface lease on private land. "Well, I know you do give subsurface leases, if the land is conserved in a trust. Why not do it for ours?" When the guy argued that the company was not interested in a subsurface lease on such a large parcel, Tom replied, "So you say you only give subsurface leases for fewer than fifteen acres? Then why not treat this as three fifteen-acre plots?" And so on and so on.

The representative phoned us with a verbal offer a few days later: five hundred dollars per acre and 12.5 percent royalties. Tom was clearly not pleased with the amount, but he had gotten a subsurface lease agreement.

He tried once more, "You already have the well dug nearby. You wouldn't drill on our site, anyway. Why not give us the amount you are giving our neighbors who surround the site—the $2,500?"

The representative wouldn't agree.

Tom paused, but told him to send the paperwork. Though proud of Tom's negotiating skills, I was beginning to wonder if compromising my values for a total of $25,000, minus about a third that amount in taxes, was worthwhile.

Next Tom asked Owlett, our attorney, to review the lease, but somehow the deal stalled. We learned that the energy company had been purchased by a major oil company, and that the takeover needed to be complete before any other action was initiated. I told Owlett, when I finally did speak to him, that I guessed we were out of any gas-lease deals. Owlett disagreed. They are pooling the land around the well site, and we could still be a part of it.

He also told me that the leases were being 'tied-up.' Leases are for five-year periods, and unless the company begins to drill, they need to be renewed, with new signing bonuses to sweeten the deal. If the company begins to drill, the lease is automatically extended indefinitely and is therefore not renewable. Presumably the lease holder will soon receive royalties, so another signing bonus won't be missed.

If the company initiates the drilling, even if only by installing a cement well pad, the lease is extended. If such a well pad exists, neither future renegotiation of the lease amount or royalty percent, nor a new lease signing bonus is possible. Making changes every five years to each and every deed is an enormous amount of work and costs the company money on many fronts. Preventing wiser landowners from banding together and negotiating better bonuses and royalty percentages is smart business, so the gas companies 'tie up' the leases.

The company decided to pool the land northwest and southeast of us for a well that was dug last August. Owlett sent an outline of the pool, superimposed over the county maps. It was a rectangle with a tooth cut out where our land is. Why not add our subsurface land to the 'rectangle' they had established? I don't know.

The company did send us the original (surface included) lease from over a year ago, not the subsequent (subsurface only) lease that Tom had negotiated and had already been reviewed by our attorney.

Tom put in a call to the gas drilling representative, who told Tom that they may 'punch another smaller hole' nearby, and so they wished to preserve our relatively large tract as a potential drilling site. We would be on a northwest/southeast rectangular pool adjacent to the one just formed. Tom explained that I would not allow a surface lease. The gas-lease guy indicated that they would not allow a subsurface lease on fifty acres.

Tom was right; we were out of the money.

Two Years Later: Concerns

The secret is this: strength lies solely in tenacity.

—Louis Pasteur

February, 2011

I received an e-mail with a forwarded video attachment from my friend, Mike Gallo. Mike has been a busy man these days. He married in January, now lives in New York City, and has a new job. It isn't his style to forward stuff, but this was from John Adgate, who had been a fellow student with me in the Human Exposure Assessment program at the medical school. I haven't been following Adgate's whereabouts, but Mike mentioned at the wedding that John had taken a department chair position at the University of Colorado.

I clicked on the attachment, since my little Michael was busy with his coloring book. It was a news report about natural gas drilling. Ever since I told everyone that I wanted to write a book about the dilemma I was facing—reasoning that if I told enough people, I would feel compelled to finish it in order to preserve my dignity—my friends are quick to notify me when anything about gas-drilling hits the news. When the *Gaslands* documentary hit the scene, my inbox was crowded with messages. The unintended consequence of everyone's solicitude is that my anxiety soars.

My stomach felt tied in knots when I heard that there was a movie about a man from Pennsylvania who had been offered a gas lease and began researching the industry. I knew I had been scooped. I had tried so hard to type at night, after the kids were in bed, but my work had progressed slowly. Still, I decided to continue my own manuscript, because, though placed in a similar situation, our approach was different: Josh Fox had gone out into the world to discover the physical causes of the ill effects of drilling; I, confined at home, had been more introspective, examining the ethical dilemmas.

Today's news slapped me hard. The newscasters for the *New York Times* were actually interviewing John Adgate! And not only that, Adgate was wearing a suit and tie, which is a far cry from what he wore in his grad school days in the lab. I was a bit shocked at the fact that he was researching the very thing that concerned me most—the potential adverse health effects resulting from emissions from gas drilling. What a disparity between us! He is at the top of our field; I am sitting at home suffering from brain atrophy.

These thoughts were bouncing in my skull as I rubbed my hands together and stalked past Michael, who was sitting on the floor surrounded by crayons. I looked out the window, ran my knuckles across my lips, and hurried back to the computer. My fingers bounced off the keyboard as I searched for contact information for Adgate.

I called him. He sounded as if he was trying to wake up. Shoot, I forgot about the time difference … not the best way to reacquaint myself with someone I haven't seen in ten years. Why am I so impulsive?

We discussed the complexity of the issue, and of course John is better versed than I, "When you place gas wells near residential neighborhoods, there's a good chance there will be human health ramifications. We just don't know what they will be yet.

He forwarded a one hundred and forty-six page document that he had co-authored, concerning a health index assessment for Garfield County, Colorado. I assume the concerns will be similar for Wellsboro, PA, but I was only able to skim a few pages; Michael was losing interest in the crayons.

The government was monitoring six of the sixty identified chemicals being emitted, and although none of them were registering at alarming levels, there could be synergistic effects.

Synergism is a word that turns the hair of environmental health scientists prematurely gray: it throws about ten wrenches of complexity into any risk assessment. The word itself means that the sum of the parts could be greater than the whole. For drilling emissions, here are some questions: What happens when children breathe 'safe' levels of several chemicals for years? What happens when the children are breathing chemicals spewing from multiple wells? Does the wind blow only some of them into their lungs? How do you calculate all this exposure?

Other than these emerging health questions about its chemical emissions, gas drilling is becoming an even more complex issue, two years from the outset of the signing frenzy in Pennsylvania. While at first everyone cheerfully saw dollar signs, they are now observing that there is a downside of drilling as well. *Gaslands*, the documentary, has raised public awareness of the contamination issues that go hand-in-hand with the drilling. 'Fracking' is now a household word. Heavy truck traffic is clogging small, two-stoplight towns and tractor-trailers hauling wide loads over winding back roads are also part of the scenery. Spills and water contamination issues are in the news, and vehicular accidents on those back roads must be taxing the emergency response teams.

License plates from Texas and Utah are common sights on trucks of men who are temporarily on the job here in

Pennsylvania. The money may be good, but these men are not here to assimilate into the community; they arrive without families. Last summer, a late-night brawl between two drilling workers ended in a murder in Wellsboro. I think that northern Pennsylvania is becoming the Wild West.

I worry about worker safety. Heavy machinery can be dangerous, and some of the men I have observed in my lifetime have few qualms about short-circuiting safety features. Reading Adgate's reports, I am even more frightened for them, for their lungs. They are right on top of the emissions. I hope, like Dad always said, that these men are looking out for Number One when it comes to safety.

Epilogue

When the gas-leasing and drilling nightmare first encroached on my farm retreat, I suspected a malignant plan of evil and savored hopes that it would all disappear, allowing us to revert back to our happy little existence, alone in our part of the world. However, the gas industry is here to stay. It behaves like any well-run business: following the letter of the law while using its influence and money to further its best interests. There are people and not-for-profit groups actively engaged in working to minimize the adverse impacts. I, however, am not one of them; I am at home: baking, doing laundry, raising my boys.

It is not all bad. I am gladdened by the sight of old Pennsylvania barns that were long deteriorating being repaired, painted, and returned to their original glory. Never before have farmers had the money to renovate such structures, and the freshness of the buildings is lovely. True, gas industry machinery clutters the background when I view many of these farms, but those should disappear. Northern Pennsylvania is looking much more prosperous.

Two years after this all started, Tom is working half-time for one of the doctors who split from the old company. Consequently, Tom golfs more than ever, though he claims it is not enough. He holds his gas-lease sacrifice loftily over my head each time he shoulders his new, handmade, all-leather, monogrammed golf bag and heads for the golf course.

Despite still purchasing organic food and many golf accessories, we do not spend more than Tom earns each month. We had another big garden haul this year—lots of potatoes, onions and peppers; I made our own elderberry jelly, froze three gallons of our own peaches, and have more pumpkin puree stored in the chest freezer than I expect to use in a lifetime.

Michael is growing quickly and happily. Matthew rides the bus—with only one transfer—and is in 'learning support' at the local public school. He is still reading way below grade level. More interested in building things than going to school, he is eternally designing windmills and solar-equipped planes and discussing his ideas with my brother, Mark.

My old car, which has been elevated in my mind as a treasure, runs pretty well, and I hope to keep it for a long time. I see it as a challenge to keep the car operating for another few years, and anyway, I would rather funnel money into things other than a new car.

As I finish this manuscript, I am struck by the irony that I vowed not to take on another full-time job while raising children, and yet here I sit, long after midnight, typing frantically at the computer, my left eye twitching involuntarily. I felt compelled to save these memories for my sons and to follow my writing dream. Perhaps any woman who loves all her jobs cannot help but keep attempting to do them all, exhausted though she may be.

I had only wanted to write about myself as a heroine, but now I ask myself if I am in fact the heroine of my story. I believe that I will never allow a drilling rig to be put on my farm, no matter the outside pressure. In contemplating my situation, I captured memories of my dad and the farm on paper. In those respects, I am content.

The energy companies provide a product that I seek, namely natural gas, so I was dismayed to discover that I am guilty—if not directly—of damaging the ground, water, and air. I am culpable as the end-user of what is gathered in the process. My resistance was a clear case of kneejerk NIMBY: Not-In-My-Backyard. I deplored the techniques of acquiring fossil fuel while still whole-heartedly using the fuel.

I am now attempting to curb my usage of all fossil fuels. I believe that if enough of us Americans curb our lavish behavior, not just our use of oil and gas, but our thoughtless buying, selling and junking, we might mitigate some of the environmental damage. My editor, Catherine Treadgold, summed it up well: "We know what we have to do; we are just unwilling to do it."

I dream of devising a universal formula for eco-friendly living, a formula of mathematically poetical genius that would both stun and save the world. If I couldn't do that, at least I should have included some already published guidelines for 'greener living' in this document. They are stashed somewhere among the piles that surround me. Surely I could have dug them out before this book went to press.

A heroine would have done so, despite bloodshot eyes. Instead I went sledding on the hill with my boys. Will I do it, someday? Will I ever again wear office attire and write extensive reports like Adgate's? Maybe. Today, though, I would rather give my two little boys a memory of laughing with me as we careen down the hillside on the back of their sled. Tomorrow I will definitely question and assess the value of risking a second fracture to my spine, and I might perhaps pick up other neglected dreams. But not today.

> When a man dies, if he can pass along enthusiasm to his children, he has left them an estate of incalculable value.
>
> —Thomas Alva Edison

References

Weidner, Krista. Natural Gas Exploration. A Landowner's Guide to Leasing Land in Pennsylvania.

College of Agricultural Sciences, Agricultural Research and Cooperative Extension, The Pennsylvania State University, 2008.

www.naturalgas.psu.edu.

Michelle Fitz Photography

Stephanie Hamel, PhD, grew up in southeastern Pennsylvania. She earned her BS in Chemistry from Grove City College, Grove City, PA, and her MS in Chemistry from Lehigh University in Bethlehem, PA. She was employed as an organic chemist in the pharmaceutical industry by The BOC Group, Inc. and at R.W. Johnson Pharmaceutical Institute, then taught Chemistry classes part-time at various community colleges in western Pennsylvania and also at Carlow College in Pittsburgh.

Dr. Hamel returned to graduate school to study environmental health issues, earning a Joint PhD in Exposure Assessment from the University of Medicine and Dentistry of New Jersey-Robert Wood Johnson Medical School and the Department of Environmental Sciences at Rutgers University. Her thesis work involved the development of a laboratory procedure to test for bioaccessibility of heavy metals from soils. Her research was funded by a US EPA STAR

Fellowship; in 1997, Stephanie was honored at a White House reception with other recipients of this award.

Dr. Hamel performed post-doctoral research in the Department of Plant Sciences at Rutgers University. Working with the Soil Fertility Specialist for Rutgers Cooperative Extension, she developed equations to calculate lead levels in soil using the standard soil testing methods for the region.

She now resides in northeastern Pennsylvania with her husband, Tom, and their two sons. This is her first book.

You can find Dr. Hamel on the Web at:

www.hamel.coffeetownpress.com

Made in the USA
Charleston, SC
16 February 2012